BOOKS THAT BRING LIFE

BOOKS THAT BRING LIFE

Eugene W. Brice

5001 AVENUE N
LUBBOCK, TEXAS 79412
PHONE (806) 762-8094

DEDICATION

To my parents, Eugene and Carrie Brice, who brought me life

ISBN 0-937462-00-4

Printed in the United States of America

CONTENTS

PREFACE

His eyes glinted a bit as he said to his pastor in a challenging way, "We don't get enough Bible at church."

The minister had played this game before, and with eyes that met the challenge, he said, "How much Bible do you get at home?"

"At home? Bible at home? What do you mean?"

"I mean how often do you read the Bible at home? You may not always be able to choose the curriculum or set the agenda here at church—none of us can—but you surely can do that at home. How much Bible are you getting there?"

The conversation continued for awhile, complete with abundant ministerial defensiveness and lay aggressiveness. Each party tended to put the blame on the other for a scarcity of Bible study and knowledge. It seemed clear, however, that minister and layman were agreed on the basic issue: the Bible ought to be more central in life than it is. Ministers ought to make it appear more often in their preaching, and laypersons ought to study it more and find ways to apply its message to daily life.

Out of this kind of conversation came the series of sermons contained in this volume. If Christians could be made to see the rich variety of exciting and relevant truth contained in the Bible, surely they would find ways to read it more. They would not need to be badgered into doing so; they would read it gladly.

The sermons which follow deal with sixteen specific books of the Bible, nine from the Old Testament, seven from the New Testament. They include: two books from the Law (Genesis and Exodus), two books of history (Judges and Samuel), three books from the wisdom and poetic literature of the Old Testament (Job, Psalms, and Proverbs), two prophets (Amos and Jeremiah), one gospel (John), three letters from Paul (Philippians, Colossians, and Thessalonians), Acts, Peter, and the Revelation of John.

These sixteen sermons have the following three purposes:

(1) In an instructional manner, they seek to tell something of how the book came to be written and what it contains. Questions about uncertain

authorship or dating are often mentioned but not dealt with at length. The listener is referred to any good biblical commentary for exhaustive treatment of such questions.

(2) In an exhortatory manner, they seek to persuade the listener to identify the basic truths revealed in the book and then apply them to specific human situations today. Today's setting is surely different, but the human predicaments described are the same. How does the book help us today?

(3) In a very practical manner, they seek to encourage the listener to go and read the book itself. "You've heard the sermon, now read the book!" Occasionally, groups today will solicit money to be used to help smuggle Bibles into countries that prohibit their distribution. But a person who *does not* read the Bible is no better off than one who *cannot* read it. The listener is encouraged to "take and read."

This book will have value to the degree that it motivates the reader to turn from the sermon to the biblical book it describes.

I am indebted to congregations who have listened and responded to these sermons, and to co-workers who have encouraged them. I hope they play some part in bringing life to readers today.

INTRODUCTION

It was early Sunday morning at a nearby restaurant. I was drinking coffee and reading the morning paper, and listening a bit to the conversation from the next booth. The folks there were heading for the early service at their own church, and I appreciated that. It was clear that they liked their church, and I appreciated that, too. Two of the people got up to leave, and one of the remaining ones said to the woman departing, "Be sure and save me a seat beside you." The departing woman said, "I usually bring my Bible with me to church, but I forgot it today. I have found that it's the best thing to use to save a seat with. They'll ask you to move your purse or coat, but not a Bible. But I'll try to save a seat anyway." And she was gone. I was left thinking over what I had just heard, and responding to different vibrations.

Attending church—that was good. Loved their church—*that* was good. Enjoyed their friends at church—that was good, too. Usually brought Bible to church—very good. Best thing to use to save a seat with? How did I respond to *that*? Without making too much of some good person's innocent remark, we can still assert that for the Christian the Bible has better uses than this. In real, but remarkable, ways it has brought life to those who across the centuries have turned to it.

That *life* flows out of the sixty-six separate books that constitute the Bible. Christians often use the term "*the* Bible" in a monolithic sort of way, not appreciating the richness of historical setting and point of view contained in the sixty-six unique volumes it contains. Karl Barth has helped us see this by suggesting that we use our imaginations a bit. Imagine that you look out the front window of your house and see sixty-six persons out in the street excitedly looking up into the sky. Your own view is obscured so that you cannot see clearly what has caught their attention up there. Obviously, they are excited about something. Their gaze and their gestures go heavenward. What are their emotions? What are they saying? To read the Bible is to try to catch for yourself what has excited them and to try to overhear their own witness.

Leaving Barth's analogy and going a bit further, consider what a rich variety those sixty-six witnesses represent. Imagine that we opened our front door and invited them in for dinner. Who could devise a suitable seating chart for such a crew? Most of them are singles, but there are seven sets of twins (I and II Samuel, Kings, Chronicles, Corinthians, Thessalonians, Timothy and Peter) and one set of triplets among them (I, II, and III John). There is the problem of language. Most (39) speak Hebrew, but many (27) speak Greek. Two are bilingual, with Ezra and Daniel moving unpredictably from Hebrew to Aramaic and back to Hebrew again. Add to that the problem of personality. Nahum is fiery and short-tempered, Jonah is humorous, Ruth romantic. Leviticus is as ponderous as an aged uncle and the Song of Solomon is almost adolescent. The later Isaiah is a friendly liberal, while Ezra is a fence-building conservative. Could anyone possibly seat Romans ("salvation by faith") next to James ("salvation by works")?

Imagine the conversations that would take place! D. T. Niles once said, "The Bible is a record of a conversation with God that went on for a long time and involved many different people. When you read it the right way, you'll find you are being drawn into that conversation."[1] These are conversations that bring us life, and each time we come to church for worship, we ought to be drawn into one of those conversations. We should no more expect to come to church without some encounter with one or more of these witnesses than we would expect to go to the opera without encountering music. The Bible is the musical score of Christian faith containing all the great themes which resound through life.

But our encounter with the Bible at church will never be enough to give us adequate knowledge or understanding of this work. If our minister decided to preach each Sunday on one chapter of the Bible, it would take almost twenty-three years to cover the 1,190 chapters that are there. We need more closeness to the Bible than we will ever be able to get at church alone. How can we get it?

The answer is obvious. All of us must do our own at-home reading and studying of the Bible if it is to come alive for us. We are, in many ways, remarkable people. We will condemn the Supreme Court for outlawing a practice in public schools which we never take advantage of at home where there are no restrictions whatsoever. Reading the Bible. whether done as a devotional exercise, a time of serious study, or a personal discipline, is open to all of us, and it leads us to life. Therefore, here is a suggestion or two or those who would start personal growth in knowledge of the Bible.

First, find yourself a good translation of the Bible. The King James Version is beautiful seventeenth century English, and especially in the Psalms, is good for devotional reading. But for real understanding, it presents difficulties. Its frequent use of such words as howbeit, peradventure, holden, aforetime, would fain, behooved, etc., make reading of the King James Version slow going indeed.

On the other extreme, The Living Bible is very easy to understand, and in many sections captures the spirit of the text superbly, but watch out! The Living Bible is *not* a translation of the Bible. It does not claim to be. It is a paraphrase, and the preface to The Living Bible acknowledges that there is a danger in paraphrasing the Scripture. "For whenever the author's exact words are not translated from the original languages, there is a possibility that the translation, however honest, may be giving the English reader something the original writer did not intend to say!"[2] Enjoy The Living Bible *as a paraphrase,* but not as a dependable translation of Scripture.

The Revised Standard Version (RSV) or the New English Bible (NEB) or the American Bible Society's Today's English Version (TEV) are all excellent translations, and I commend them to you for serious reading and study of the Bible. Even these should be in sturdy editions that encourage note taking in margins, and printed in a form that encourages reading. Imagine trying to read an Agatha Christie story where each sentence was numbered, indented and printed in narrow columns two to a page and between the two columns a little alley runs, containing cross references to other Agatha Christie stories. Yet this is exactly what many editions do to the books of the Bible.

The first step, then, is to find a good translation of the Bible, helpfully printed and arranged.

Having found a good translation, consider a second suggestion. *Read it!* One of Charles Schultz' little characters in "Peanuts" makes this profound statement: "I think I've made one of the first steps in unveiling the mysteries of the Old Testament. I'm starting to read it."[3] Amazing, isn't it, that many of us will attend classes about the Bible and listen to sermons about the Bible and see programs about the Bible, but we won't read it!

Some time ago, the Book of the Month Club sent out a survey to its membership. The survey listed a number of recent books and asked beside each title, "Have you read this book?" The editors were fascinated by the reply of one member. "Not personally," he answered. How else can you read a book, other than personally? He probably meant that he had seen the book, had heard it discussed, and knew its main thesis, but that he, personally, had never gotten around to reading it.

This is exactly where many of us find ourselves in relation to the Bible. We read it every way but personally. Because of this, our second suggestion is disarmingly simple: read it!

But where do you start? Suggestion number three says, *Start with an individual Bible book in its entirety.* Pick out a book of history, such as Judges, or of wisdom, such as Proverbs, or a prophetic book like Amos. Select one of the gospels, or a particular letter of Paul. Find out its probable date, its setting in the context of biblical history, its probable author, and the issues it was written to address.

Then, with this background, read the book carefully. Note its chief characters, the heroes and the villains. Note new ideas that emerge from the book, and how different people responded to them. Note peculiarities of language and style, poetic images and figures used. Try to get an understanding of what this one book says, and speculate a bit on how it must have been received in its own day. Who would likely have objected to it? What arguments would it have produced?

The emphasis here is on the complete book, not on some well-known or controversial passage it might contain. Much of our Bible study is piecemeal. Yet, we would have difficulty understanding a person who is interested in English literature sitting down and reading eight lines from Shakespeare, two from John Donne, a half page of Winston Churchill, and a line of Keats. We land so lightly on isolated parts of biblical books that we miss an understanding of the whole. So, start with a particular book. The sermons contained in this volume are intended to whet the appetite for just that approach.

Finally, take what you have learned from that book and shine it right down on your own life. What does it reveal about your own condition as a child of God?

The serious student of the Bible today quickly recognizes a collection of names, dates, facts, and figures about the Bible, but personal meaning must be inserted by the student. It is not enough to know only the characters and chronology of the Bible. In 1718, a fellow cast in prison in Amsterdam is said to have used his empty time to collect some facts about the Bible: how many books, chapters, and verses it contained, how many times the word God appears, which verse is longest, shortest, and which is the middle verse of the Bible. You may or may not need to know that the King James Version of the Bible contains 3,565,480 letters. That kind of information may have curiosity value, but it does not bring life.

The names and dates and places of the Bible are simply the clothing worn by the great truths of God's reach for his children. Underneath the surface facts are the great truths about the meaning of life itself.

A theologian and an astronomer once chanced to sit together on a plane. On learning the theologian's line of work, the astronomer said brusquely, "Do unto others as you would have them do unto you—that's my theology." The theologian answered just as quickly, "Twinkle, twinkle little star—that's my astronomy." There is something more to Christian theology than the Golden Rule, just as there is much more to astronomy than "Twinkle, twinkle little star."

The result of good, open reading of the Bible is to catch a glimpse of that "something more." It has been suggested that the Bible is like a window on our house. If we look *at* the window, we see dust and fly specks and cracks. If we look *through* the window we can see all the reality of the world we live in. If we look narrowly *at* the Bible, our vision becomes limited, but if we look through it to see the reality of God's love for us, what wideness of vision it brings. The New Testament itself puts it well: "For the word of God is alive and active. . . . It sifts the purposes and thoughts of the heart." (Heb. 4:12 NEB) And it brings us life.

The challenge, then, is to take these books and read them. Learn from them, and let them renew your life. Look through them to God's will for your life. Listen in on their conversations and hear the sound of their music.

A man once took his New Testament to the bookbinder for repair work. It was a family treasure, one which meant a lot to the owner. The bookbinder put an entirely new leather cover on the small volume, and then discovered that there was not enough room on the spine to print the words "The New Testament." He simply abbreviated the words, and the owner received his small book back from the bookbinder with the simple cover letters, "T.N.T." And that's what it is! The New Testament, T.N.T., the word of God, ready to blow away old weakness and sin and put in its place a new relationship with the God who offers his people life. It is one of his greatest gifts to us, these books that bring life.

1 GENESIS
In the Beginning

How much should the first sentence tell? Novelists often say that the first sentence, the very beginning of a novel, is hardest to write because in some very subtle way it ought to hint at all that is going to follow. Here are some first sentences from famous books. Can you guess which books they are?

"The great fish moved silently through the night waters." *Moby Dick* by Melville? No, that is the first line of the recently popular novel called *Jaws.*[1] Here's another: "It was morning, and the new sun sparkled gold across the ripples of a gentle sea." That's from *Jonathan Livingston Seagull.*[2] "He lay flat on the brown pine needled floor of the forest." Ernest Hemingway began *For Whom the Bell Tolls* with this sentence.[3]

"In the beginning God created the heavens and the earth." (Gen. 1:1) The author is God, and the book is Genesis, and implicit in those understated words is all that follows in the drama of God's reach for his people. Genesis is the book of beginnings, one which brings light and life to any person who reaches for some personal moment of new beginning.

Look first at the scope of this book which begins our Bible. It starts with the majestic story of the creation of the world, and quickly tells of the creation of God's people to dwell in it. The stories of Adam and Eve and their brief stay in Eden follow, then the tragic story of the brothers, Cain and Abel. Next comes the story of Noah and the Flood and the Tower of Babel incident. With the eleventh chapter of the book, the history of the Jewish people begins as the family of Abraham is called out of the land of Ur. On to the Promised Land they come. The remaining chapters tell of Abraham's descendants, of Isaac and Rebekah, of grandson Jacob and his twin brother Esau, of Joseph and his eleven brothers. The book ends with the tribes of Israel living in Egypt and moving slowly toward slavery under the Egyptian Pharaoh.

So the historical drama which led centuries later to Jesus Christ was begun. Genesis is a book of beginnings, one that seeks to explain how it is that certain things are as they are. Scholars call these stories "etiologies," explanations of how things began. Why do snakes crawl on their bellies? Why do women suffer at childbirth? Why must men work and sweat and strain? Why is there a rainbow? Why are there many different languages? Why is there a special relationship between the Jewish people and God?

Genesis is an exciting book, and a good place for any person to begin a discipline of Bible reading. It is a book full of information about the first experiences of humanity, the first struggling steps toward God. But it gives us more than information. It gives us insight into the nature of our life in this world God has created for us.

For example, consider these observations from the book, and see what God is telling us through them:

- In the beginning, Genesis tells of Eve, the first wife, living in the paradise of Eden. But it soon tells of Eve being the first woman to be dissatisfied with what she had and the first to reach out for something she didn't need and shouldn't ask for.

- In the beginning, Genesis tells of Adam, the first, heroic husband. But it soon tells of this noble man being the very first to blame his wife for something he did of his own free will.

- In the beginning, Genesis tells of the good and holy gift of sexual relationships, but long before the book ends it has told of rape and incest and adultery.

- In the beginning, Genesis tells us of Cain, the first person born on this earth, the first son, the first to enjoy the rich relationship with a younger brother. But then, with dramatic suddenness, Genesis tells us of Cain being the first murderer as he takes the life of his brother, Abel.

- Noah, says Genesis, had the distinction of being the first vinegrower, the first maker of wine, in all the world. But then the book adds the story of how Noah was the very first person to bring disgrace upon himself as he lay in a drunken stupor. Noah, the first vinegrower, was the first drunkard on earth.

- Tubal-Cain was the first forger of metals, says Genesis, but before the book ends swords and spears were being forged.

- In the beginning, Genesis tells of the very first nations emerging in strength on the face of the earth, but long before the book ends it has told of the first bloody and cruel wars being fought.

Do you see, then, what all this implies? Implicit in every beginning is the possibility of both success and failure. God didn't write the final chapter as he wrote the opening sentence. *God gives the beginning, but then the story can go either way,* and which way it will go is never apparent at the beginning. Christopher Morley has a poem that expresses this in another way. It is entitled "No Coaching," and goes like this:

I went to the theatre
With the author of the successful play.
He insisted on explaining everything,
Told me what to watch, the details of direction,
The errors of the property man, the foibles of the star.
He anticipated all my surprises, and ruined the evening.
Never again! And mark you,
The Greatest Author of all made no such mistake![4]

The end result is never obvious from the beginning. Implicit in every beginning is uncertainty, because God has given us the greatest, most magnificent, and yet most dangerous gift of all—freedom!

Freedom is a dangerous gift because it puts the burden of choice on us, and it includes the possibility of both success and failure. Early in 1982, a movie executive went to the M&M Company and said that they would like to use those little candies, M&Ms, in a movie they were making—something about visitors from outer space who, in the movie, would like candy. No, said the M&M vice-president, he didn't want his product used in that way. So the movie "exec" went to the company that makes Reece's Pieces, and they accepted the offer, and in that phenomenally successful movie, "E.T.," the little space child is lured out of hiding by a trail of Reece's Pieces instead of M&Ms. Reece's stock has gone up several fold as a result, and an M&M vice-president has been looking for a job. Implicit in every new opportunity—success and failure. Freedom is a wide and risky river. Freedom to love means freedom to hate and kill. Freedom to choose the good means freedom to grasp the evil. Freedom to subdue the earth means freedom to pillage it. Genesis shines light on this from every angle, as it tells stories of men and women who faced choices and used their freedom, some to destroy their life, some to fulfill it.

Do you see how this truth permeates every level of your life? We face new beginnings, exciting beginnings. All the raw materials for joy and fulfillment are there. But so also is that dangerous gift of freedom. We are free to make of every new beginning exactly what we will.

When two people come together in marriage, for example, it is a beginning full of great promise, yet one full of uncertainty. Their love is real.

Yes, to be sure, but so is their freedom. And because of it, wrong choices can be made, and how quickly they can be turned out of their paradise!

We acknowledge this in our wedding ceremonies, although in the excitement and delight of the moment, we often do not hear the words we are saying. "For better or for worse," we say, "for richer or for poorer, in sickness and in health, to love and to cherish." This is our promise. In Orthodox Jewish weddings, the bride and groom at a certain point in the ceremony drink from a small, delicate glass of wine to symbolize the joy of their life together. But then, they take the glass, place it on the floor, and under their feet they crush the glass into pieces, a symbol of the possibility of sadness and misfortune as their life together unfolds.

Implicit in every new beginning is uncertainty. God has given us freedom, and it means that at home we can climb just as high or sink just as low as we in our freedom choose.

In another area, there is often a rosebud on the pulpit in church, a symbol of a new life that has come to the church family. In dedication services for parents and infants, the rosebud is handed out. It represents a beginning. It must unfold in its own good time, and it depends on the nurture of loving hands in order to realize its potential. As parents we have freedom to deal with those newly begun lives as we will.

Carl Sandburg told of two men exchanging gossip in a general store in Hardin County, Kentucky, one day in February, 1809. "Anything happen over the last week?" one asks. "No," answers the other, "nothing's happened. Oh, 'cept there's a new baby down to Tom Lincoln's house. A boy, I think." *Beginnings!* Beginnings. And implicit in every one of them is success or failure. As parents of young children, ours is the freedom to do with them just as we will. Everything we do, everything we say with regard to them—in what soft clay it is written!

Say it again. Implicit in every new beginning is a measure of uncertainty, for God has created us free. Then in this context, we face new beginnings. What will they be? Which choices will we make?

Given the gift of freedom and the gift of life itself, is there any one of us who can afford not to take Jesus Christ as his or her guide in the year to come? The road will be uncertain, yes, but Jesus said, "I am the way,. . . ." (John 14:6) The night will often be dark, yes, but he said, "I am the light. . . ." (John 8:12) Oftimes there will seem no way out of our predicaments, but he said, "I am the door. . . ." (John 10:9)

Genesis warns us that freedom is a dangerous gift, but in Christ, God offers us a way of using freedom. Is there any better way for you and me in the year to come? Louise Haskins put it well:

"And I said to the man who stood
at the gate of the year:
Give me a light, that I may tread
safely into the unknown!"
And he replied:
"Go out into the darkness and put
thine hand into the Hand of God;
That shall be to thee better than light,
and safer than a known way."[5]

2 EXODUS
Free At Last!

Free at last! Do you recall the exultation and inner relief we all felt when the American hostages stepped off that plane and were home from Iran? Their captivity was over! How many days had it been since that angry mob invaded the American embassy, and in one awful moment, freedom was gone for fifty-two innocent people?

The interplay between freedom and captivity has always been a recurring theme in our lives, whether dealing with politics or religion or personal discipline. At times we are free, and at times we are captive, in such a variety of ways. And the most fascinating aspect to it involves the different ways freedom can be lost. For some, it is lost in one loud moment of unlawful violence, but for most of us the loss of freedom involves a much slower process.

A woman on a radio talk show was discussing her intention to stop smoking. She was thirty-five, she said, and had smoked since she was fourteen. But as she thought back on her problem, she wondered aloud just when she had been captured by this smoking habit. She was a slave to it now, but once she had not been. "Exactly when did I lose my freedom?" she asked. "How long did it take me to realize that I was a slave to it?"

I thought of the book of Exodus when she said this, because in that book we learn that it took the Jewish people 400 years to realize that their vacation in Egypt had turned into slavery. When the book of Genesis closes, the Israelites were living in great honor in Egypt, with Joseph as the Pharaoh's right-hand man. But when Exodus opens 400 years later, a Pharaoh who "knew not Joseph" had come to power, and the Israelites were living in slavery.

The book of Exodus tells what happens when the Israelites finally realized that they were honored guests no longer. They were slaves, their freedom gone. It is an exciting book, one which rings with themes as modern as today. Here is a quick summary of what the reader finds in this ancient book which brings life:

It begins by telling of the Israelites' plight in Egypt, and of the birth of Moses (chapter 1). There comes quickly the story of the baby Moses placed on the water in the bullrushes, of how he was found and adopted by the daughter of Pharaoh (chapter 2). Moses was raised in the royal palace of Egypt, but when he killed an Egyptian soldier while defending a fellow Israelite he was forced to run away. He lived as a shepherd in Midian until God called him to go back to Egypt and lead his people out of slavery (chapter 3).

With his brother Aaron, Moses did just that. The book tells of their struggle for freedom and of the plagues that came on Egypt (chapters 4-12). Then comes the story of the people crossing the Red Sea as it parted before them (chapter 14) and how they were fed by manna as they wandered in the wilderness (chapter 16). Then God makes a covenant with this wandering people, and in Exodus 20 the Ten Commandments are given and the law established. The remaining twenty chapters of the book deal with detailed Jewish civil and criminal law, and make for hard reading. The first twenty chapters contain the heart of the story and offer exciting reading.

Most Jewish people even today consider this book as the most important in their Bible, for it tells of the birth of the Jewish nation. And out of Exodus comes themes that still live in both Jewish and Christian religion. The Jewish Passover meal was begun in Exodus, the practice out of which comes our service of Communion. The idea of a Messiah, a Savior sent from God, originates with the Moses story, as all through later Jewish history the people are looking for a *new* Moses to free them from despair. Many of the exciting themes that come later in the Bible begin with the book of Exodus. It is an exciting book, one full of drama and adventure, and it reaches across these 3,000 years to speak to us today. What does it say?

It tells us that it is quite possible for children of God to be living in slavery and yet never realize it! At first, Egypt was the salvation of the tribes of Israel, giving them food in time of famine. So slowly were the chains slipped on that they hardly realized they had been made captive. We learn from this book that every person ought constantly to be aware of what is slowly taking command of his or her life. It is possible for any of us to be living in slavery to a particular habit or life-style and never really know how and when it all began.

Patterns of living in a marriage can become enslaving. We didn't intend it to turn out this way. We don't really know how or when we got caught in this tight little cell of brusqueness and silence and tension, but one day we look at ourselves, and for the first time we note the bars and see the thickness of the walls about us. We are in prisons of our own making! We let little patterns of cruelty and thoughtlessness harness our acting and speaking, and often are not aware of the vicious circle of resentment that enslaves us at home.

Some of us, without being aware it is happening, let our possessions enslave us, shutting down those impulses toward generosity that once were strong within us. We are not sure when and how that happened, but happen it did. Many of us remember our earlier days and are led to this kind of remark: "You know, if someone had told me twenty years ago that I would be making as much money as I am now, I wouldn't have believed it. If I made that much money, I would have said that giving generously to the church would be easy. I would tithe my income and hardly notice it, so much would be left over. But now that I am making this much money, I can't afford a tithe! In fact, the only way I could afford it would be if God reduced my income! How did that happen? When did I get like this?" Say it again: we move slowly into slavery to our possessions, and those who find it impossible to be good stewards may not hear the chains rattling, but they're there, nonetheless.

Some become slaves to bitterness and resentment. They do not realize what has enslaved them until they become aware of how easily offended they are, how people have come to expect complaint and despair from them. The chains of negativism fall about some very devout people. They are in slavery and often quite unaware of it.

This book waves a warning flag at us. Watch out, it says, for you can lose your freedom and not really know it. Slowly, the chains of some deadly life-style may come in place, and the years may pass in unconscious slavery. This was what happened to the people of Israel in Egypt, until God said, "Go down, Moses," and Moses went down, and out of Egypt came the slave people of Israel. Free at last!

The book of Exodus tells us something else. The Israelites discovered, somewhat to their surprise, *that absolute, unrestricted freedom is but another kind of captivity.* They discovered this while wandering around in aimless freedom in the wilderness. How long they had looked forward to this moment when Egypt would be far away and they would be free. That moment had finally come, but now, the freedom they longed for had turned to frustration and despair. How did Isaiah put it? ". . .the twilight I longed for has been turned for me into trembling." (Isaiah 21:4)

A teacher in a modern preschool used a particular psychological approach in letting her students have complete freedom in the class. They could play at whatever they wanted to, day after day. Finally, one youngster approached her with the valid complaint, "I'm tired of doing whatever I want to do." For fulfillment and satisfaction, order and discipline are necessary. Complete, unrestricted freedom is, of all things, least satisfying in the long run.

Most young people have difficulty believing this. If you are one, perhaps you see yourself as an Israelite, still living in captivity under some stern Pharaoh, captive to a particular house and family, and you would like to cross some Red Sea to freedom. The only difference may be that *your* Pharaoh may be as eager to see you go as you are! But you will discover that whether the orders come from outside you (parents and teachers) or from inside you, some order or discipline will be necessary to give you real satisfaction in life.

In the case of the Israelites, it was the Law which came to give them discipline and order. Paul says that the Law was the schoolteacher, helping the people find the way to life. Bishop Kennedy tells of the newly arrived preacher in town who asked the small boy the way to the post office. The boy gave him directions and the minister thanked him, saying, "You come to church next Sunday and I'll show you the way to heaven." The boy shook his head doubtfully. "How can you show me the way to heaven," he asked, "when you can't even find the post office?"[1]

The law showed the Israelites the way to heaven; that is, the way to perfect and use their freedom. Real freedom always requires discipline in order to be meaningful. Any young man is free to play on the football team. But suppose he goes to the coach and says, "Coach, I'm willing to play halfback on the team and I'll be there for the kickoff, but don't expect me for practice after school." We know what the coach would say. The freedom to play on the team depends on the willingness to accept the chains of discipline.

Real freedom must always find direction. You decide where you want to go and then determine what kind of discipline will get you there. Do you want the love you know in your marriage to be absolutely unique and special? Then your freedom is drastically limited! A wedding ring, someone has said, is a little metal band that cuts off circulation! Fences are put up, and you accept a promise of faithfulness as the price to be paid for what you want.

The Israelites found their complete freedom in the desert to be worthless until the Law came to give direction to their freedom. If Exodus teaches us that it is possible to lose our freedom without realizing it, it also teaches that freedom, to be creative and productive, must be guided by some gladly accepted discipline.

One last point: Exodus ends with the people of Israel still in the wilderness, the Promised Land with its milk and honey yet to come. Exodus tells only the beginning of a story. *Freedom has been won, but it was still not clear what the people would do with it.* As the book concludes, this issue remains unsettled. So it is with our own journey of faith. Whatever our captivity, Jesus Christ comes to open the door and let us out. ". . .and you will know the truth," he said, "and the truth will make you free." (John 8:32) But what next? Free to do what?

During the years we served in Puerto Rico, we lived right next door to a genial professor named Lopez. A man of about 55, Professor Lopez had always wanted to play the piano, and a year or so before we arrived he finally found himself free to study music. He bought a piano and began lessons. Living in the tropics, without air conditioning of any kind, we were in completely open houses. Day after day, hour after hour, the notes of Professor Lopez' scales came through our windows. Scales, arpeggios, scales, C, F, B-flat, over and over again. For three years we heard Lopez' scales. He used his freedom to take lessons and accepted the hard discipline of practicing, but somehow the music never came! Only scales! That has been many years ago, but I suspect that somewhere tonight back in the mountains of Puerto Rico as the moon rises through the flamboyant trees, the sounds of the major and minor scales may still be heard, unless Professor Lopez has found the courage to make music out of his freedom and discipline.

Exodus tells how God brought freedom to the people of Israel, and gave to them the discipline of law, and then the rest of the Bible tells of the music Israel made as a result. This book raises questions for us, questions that bring life. (1) Have we become slaves without knowing it? What master do we unknowingly serve? (2) Is our personal freedom guided by any kind of self-accepted discipline? Have we accepted Jesus Christ as the master of our lives, leading us out of the wilderness? (3) And finally, if we have, indeed, claimed Christ as the perfector of our freedom, do our lives produce the music of joy and faithfulness?

Your opportunity every day is to move out of slavery into service. You can do it right now, for you see, whatever the slavery of your past might have been, in the sight of God you have a spotless future.

3 JUDGES
The Ups and Downs of Devotion

Hanging in the youth center of the church is a banner that has on it these words: "Thank God for your downs! They make your ups seem upper." If you are a person who has no ups and downs, the book of Judges will not seem real to you. Possibly, there are people who live life on a perfectly level plain, never wavering between high and low moments. The level they maintain may be up or down. They may live forever in the penthouse or forever in the cellar. One husband was described by his wife in this way: "He has a very even temper. He stays mad all the time."

If you are among those very few who have no ups and downs in life, you may have difficulty understanding the book of Judges, for it is a book of wavering between highs of devotion and lows of disobedience.

In this book, the spirit of Israel is on an unending seesaw. In one historical situation, it is surprisingly high. In the next, it is discouragingly low. One moment, the people are strong. The next moment they are weak. One moment they are righteous and obedient; the next, sinful and unruly.

When does all this wavering take place? The book of Judges covers a period of some two hundred years in Old Testament history. Remember that the Exodus from Egypt under Moses came about 1300 BC and that the first great king of Israel, David, began to rule about 1000 BC. Judges describes the chaotic history of Israel between about 1220 BC and 1020 BC, after the people of Israel arrived in the Promised Land but before they established the monarchy.

It was a period of dramatic ups and downs. Here is a passage that succinctly describes the era: "Whenever the Lord raised up judges for them, the Lord was with the judge, and he saved them from the hand of their enemies all the days of the judge. . . . But whenever the judge died, they turned back and behaved worse than their fathers. . . ." (Judges 2:18-19)

In the twenty chapters which follow, the author describes in detail this process of wavering back and forth between obedience and disobedience. There is, as the old Hollywood film makers used to say, a cast of thousands. The villains are the hostile people around Israel: the Philistines, Phoenicians, Moabites, Ammonites, and others. The heroes are the judges God raised up to lead his people. By far, the best known of these was Samson, the Hebrew hippie, long-haired and unorthodox, the man of great strength who finally, blind and desperate, pulled down the Philistine temple upon himself and his captors. (Judges 14-16)

Twelve such judges are described. Deborah is the one woman among them, and others are: Othniel, Ehud, Gideon, Abimelech, Tola, Jair, Jephthah, Ibzan, Elon, and Abdon. There is much violence in the book. Its rating today would require "Parental Guidance," because of the presence of brutal murders in almost every chapter. Murder, assassination, and massacre are taken-for-granted facts of life in this period of history.

But the characteristic of the book which stands out most clearly is that one already mentioned, the ups and downs of the people of Israel. What an incredible amount of wavering between obedience and disobedience, strength and weakness! Read through the book and find repeated time after time this key verse: "And the people of Israel *again* did what was evil in the sight of the Lord. . . ." (Judges 2:11, 3:7, 12, 4:1, 6:1, 10:6, 13:1, etc. [Italics added]) The verses which follow tell in detail of the trouble Israel found herself in because of her repeated sin. The writer then tells how God raised up a judge to lead Israel, how he or she (Deborah!) fought and won the battle. But after a time that judge would die, and very shortly there comes again the familiar verse, "And the people of Israel again did what was evil in the sight of the Lord."

Twelve times in the book that cycle is repeated: obedience and prosperity, then a slipping away and sin, then disaster, then restoration through a strong judge, then obedience and prosperity, followed by slipping away. The book of Judges gives us a clear picture of the ups and downs of Israel's devotion in these two centuries about a thousand years before the birth of Jesus.

It seems quite clear that the book describes not only a period in Hebrew history, *but also a pattern of human conduct which is familiar to any generation.* Ups and downs of devotion! What wavering between good and evil we do. The old spiritual puts it well: "Sometimes I'm up, sometimes I'm down, oh yes, Lord." How quickly and inevitably we move from one to the other.

The waverings of the Hebrew people under the judges serves as a mirror for our own spiritual wandering. Surely the pattern is familiar to us. We find life tumbling in about us for any one of a variety of reasons. We have blundered grievously and we are suffering for our sins. Through a process of self-judgment, we come to ourselves. We get the reins of life back into our own hands, and through hard discipline we regain integrity. Our life is then blessed by God because our lives are under control again. Whatever that thing might be—our tendency to drink too much, our quick tempers, our loose tongues, our moodiness—we get it under control and we are blessed. Life has a ring to it, a joy. But then we get careless. It is not that we don't know better. We do! But we get careless, and the same old enemy comes invading our lives again, and ". . .the people of Israel again did what was evil in the sight of the Lord." Ups and downs!

Why is this? How is it that we can be strong one moment and weak the next? Paul, the first century Christian missionary, wondered about this. "I do not understand my own actions. For I do not do what I want, but I do the very thing I hate. . . . I can will what is right, but I cannot do it." (Romans 7:15, 18) It *is* hard to understand. Here is an unknown mother writing in poetry the feelings of many of us:

March came in like a lion, Lord, like I do some days;
I storm and glower and huff and puff, lots of bluster and blow and bluff,
Lots of snarl at those I love, iron hands, no velvet glove.
And then, next day, like March's lamb, it's aimless and witless and weak I am.
No discipline, no rules, no aim. Can the lion and lamb both be the same?
Can one become two? And if I do, does it keep the children guessing who?
Is Mom a lion today, or a lamb? Oh Lord, I don't know what I am.
I only know that I'd like to be a stable, responsible, rational me.[1]

Good one day and bad the next! Patient and in control one week, but the next week irascible and reckless. We see ourselves clearly mirrored in the ups and downs of Israel's devotion.

As we remember how the Hebrews suffered terribly when they turned from good to evil, *we see that this is exactly what we have learned about life itself.* No matter how good our intentions are, we must stick with the good we know. Turn loose of it, and we suffer. How easily we get sidetracked with our very best resolutions. We start out a day saying we are going to be patient, and before the first gurgle of the percolator we are shouting at someone we love. Today we are going to be kind, but before the cereal has had time to snap, much less crackle or pop, we have reverted to our unloving selves. How quickly our ups become downs!

The father sits down one evening firmly intending to have a friendly, understanding conversation with his teenage son. He has read Dr. Ginnott's books about open acceptance between parents and teenagers, and he has read Dr. Harris' books about OK-ness. Those fellows are right, and the father knows it. This time it is going to be different. This time he is going to be understanding and patient and creative. So he smiles confidently and in a gentle voice says, "Son, you think maybe this month you ought to get a haircut?" Good intentions, self-control, and understanding abound. But ten minutes later, angry son is stomping out of the room as red-faced father shouts, "*Why* are you going to get a haircut tomorrow? Because I'm your father, that's why!" Ups and downs!

Dr. Haim Ginnott tells of such a conversation. "Once in a blue moon, almost every parent hears his son or daughter declare, 'I'm stupid.' Knowing that *his* child cannot be stupid, the parent sets out to convince him that he is bright:

Son: I am stupid.

Father: You are not stupid.

Son: Yes, I am.

Father: You are not. Remember how smart you were at camp? The counselor thought you were one of the brightest.

Son: How do you know what he thought?

Father: He told me so.

Son: Yeah, how come he called me 'stupe' all the time?

Father: He was just kidding.

Son: I am stupid and I know it. Look at my grades in school.

Father: You'll just have to work harder.

Son: I already work harder and it doesn't help. I have no brains.

Father: You are smart, I know.

Son: I am stupid, *I* know.

Father: (loudly) You are not stupid.

Son: Yes, I am.

Father: You are not stupid, stupid!"[2]

Quickly and unintentionally, the climate changes in such conversations. "And the people of Israel again did what was evil in the sight of the Lord."

Or, if it is not losing control and turning aside in a specific situation, it is doing so with life in general. This is a slower and more gentle slipping away. No matter how good a man's record has been, when he turns away from it, it brings suffering on him and others. He may have been a good accountant, or lawyer, or husband for forty years, but if he turns away, he is going to suffer.

A man starts out on a marriage, and as long as he treats those promises he made with respect, he is blest. The feelings of decency and responsibility and cleanness are their own refreshing reward. The ups are up indeed. But if he reneges on his sacred vows, as sure as night follows day, he will suffer for it. Whatever a man sows, he reaps, and the downs of dishonored faithfulness are down indeed.

A woman has a problem with alcohol, and she knows what it does to her and what it makes of her. As long as she leaves it alone, she feels responsible and trustworthy, and she is. But let her give way, and she knows the midnight of despair and guilt it brings to her life.

A person pledges himself to following Jesus Christ, and through worship and service and spiritual discipline, he is a credit to that pledge. But how easy to lose sight of that high calling! Life becomes boxed in by apathy on the one hand and diversion on the other, so that the Lord is quite shunted aside. Deep down, every person who has gone from ups to downs in duty to God feels the pain of it.

What has all this said to us? As we read the book of Judges, we will see how time after time Israel went from high moments to low, turning from obedience to disobedience, and back again. We know that this is a pattern we all follow, for the ups and downs of devotion are frequently travelled trails in our own lives. We can make these conclusions:

(1) Wavering is inevitable for us. Our life will continually move from the mountain top to the valley, and back again, as the tides of the spirit move in and out.

(2) We always bring suffering on ourselves when we move from obedience to disobedience. This is a simple law of the spiritual world—that whatever we sow, we reap.

(3) Along with the suffering that comes with disobedience, the Lord always sends a way out of the valley of despair. Twelve times the people of Israel chose to disobey, but twelve times the Lord sent a way back to faithfulness again. Through the continuing presence of Jesus Christ among us, he still sends that way for us to climb up out of our downs of devotion.

4 SAMUEL
In Search of a Perfect System

It has always been easier to describe what is wrong in a nation than to prescribe a solution. Here are two classic descriptions of national ills. Can you guess what periods in world history are involved, and which nations are being described? "Things fall apart," this writer says. "The centre cannot hold. Mere anarchy is loosed upon the world." The second writer is less poetic, more matter-of-fact: "In those days. . .every man did what was right in his own eyes."

There is a remarkable timelessness about these statements. People in most generations hear these words, look at themselves, and say, "That's *our* day the writer is describing. That's *us*." The first quotation, describing the pulling apart of order, is by W. B. Yeats, who was picturing the western nations as World War I approached.[1] "Mere anarchy is loosed upon the world." The second is an unknown author's description of the people of Israel about 1060 BC when the book of Samuel opens. "In those days. . .every man did what was right in his own eyes." (Judges 21:25)

Both quotations accurately describe the basic human predicament which persists from century to century, including our own. In the midst of a culture which advises us to "do our own thing," we hear echoes across three thousand years from a people who did just that, and found it wanting. Those echoes come from the book of Samuel, one of the most readable, fast-paced books of the Bible. It is a book which describes how, in that ancient setting, the people struggled to find a system that would bring order to their lives.

The book is so long that it could not be included on one Hebrew scroll, so it was divided into two parts. It covers a 100-year slice of Hebrew history, beginning in anarchy about 1060 BC and ending with the close of David's reign as king about 960 BC. Written centuries before the Greek historian Herodotus, often called "the father of history," this book is one of the earliest examples in world literature of an objective court history of a nation.

It begins with the story of the boy Samuel and his nocturnal conversations with God. (I Sam. 2, 3) Samuel grows up to be a judge over Israel I Sam. 7) and takes part in the selection of Saul as Israel's first king (I Sam. 9). We read of Saul's wars with the Philistines (I Sam. 13), of his son Jonathan's friendship with David (I Sam. 18), of David's slaying Goliath (I Sam. 17). Saul dies in battle (I Sam. 31) and David becomes king (II Sam. 2), meets and marries Bathsheba (II Sam. 11), establishes Jerusalem as the capital (II Sam. 5), and makes Israel a strong and vigorous nation. It is a book which describes the stumbling efforts of the nation Israel to find a perfect system by which to live.

Any person who thinks seriously about his or her own nation and its integrity will find insight by a close reading of this ancient book. In it, we see the disturbing condition the people of Israel were in, the solution they devised, the problems this caused and the conclusion of the matter.

The Condition. "In that day, there was no king in Israel, and every man did what was right in his own eyes." With this verse the book of Judges closes, setting the scene for the stories of Samuel. For nearly a hundred years after the slow move into the Promised Land, the people had been led by a series of judges who sought to give them order. Charismatic-type leaders, the judges moved like skyrockets into Israel's sky, had their brief day, and were gone. There was no stability, no succession of authority, no central government. Every one did what was right *in his own eyes,* and the resulting anarchy seriously weakened the would-be nation of Israel.

Is there any level of life on which such anarchy would work? As a result of our overcrowded society and the strictures that go with it, we have a wistful yearning for complete personal freedom. The "do your own thing" approach is a result. It has a certain appeal, but most of us abandon it right quickly when the real problems of life appear. If we grow desperately ill and need quick and skilled treatment, we do not want to go to a doctor who does his own thing in medicine or who did his own thing in medical school. We want someone who has chosen to serve a discipline, who has given his or her life to systematic knowledge and truth. When our car stops running, we are poorly served by a mechanic who does what is right in his own eyes. We need one who knows what makes motors work and accepts that discipline.

Marriage does not work when we simply do whatever seems right in our own eyes. This relationship involves a deliberate, solemn renouncing of the "do your own thing" approach. "Will you keep only unto him so long as you both shall live?" "Will you keep only unto her?" "Will you forsake all others?"

No wonder Israel's people felt weak and defenseless in the midst of highly organized, tightly disciplined nations like Philistia. They needed a better system, something to govern and direct and discipline them. Obviously, their lives would be controlled by *something*. Paul said, "You belong to the power which you choose to obey." (Romans 6:16, J. B. Phillips Translation[2]) The only power the people had obeyed was anarchy, and it did not work. This was the perplexing condition for which the people sought a solution.

The Solution. Dissatisfied with the anarchy that existed, the people demanded a king. All the nations that were giving them the most trouble had kings, so this seemed the solution to their problem. They approached Samuel and said to him, ". . .we will have a king over us, that we also may be like all the nations, and that our king may govern us and go out before us *and fight our battles.*" (I Sam. 8:19, 20 [Italics added])

It sounded so easy! Discouraged by the weakness their anarchy had produced, the people romanticized the role of a prospective king. "Why didn't we think of this before? It will require nothing from us—our king will do it all. He will go out before us and fight our battles for us." Reluctantly, Samuel found Saul, a man who was "a head taller" than anyone else in Israel, and anointed him king. The perfect system had been found. The people had a king now, and their problems were over.

It did not work out that way, of course. Few easy solutions to hard questions work out. Still, we yearn for them, search for them, give ourselves to them. A botanist reveals that he is close to the development of a lawn grass that will grow two inches high, then stop growing! A book offers to tell us how to lose weight without dieting. A health center argues that two ten-minute exercise periods a week will get us in shape. A company offers a church a surefire system for raising the budget, a system that requires no work, no commitment. A couple wants to change the wedding vow to read: ". . .so long as we both shall *love.*"

Surely there is a system somewhere which will gain us our objectives without requiring anything from us. In world history, one after another form of government has been offered as the perfect system. The earliest countries devised monarchies, the Greeks favored oligarchies and plutocracies, Calvin proposed a theocracy in Geneva, democracy surfaced in the United States and France, socialism in England, communism in Russia. Each purports to be the perfect system, one which leads people to fulfillment and offers them order and stability.

Israel's solution shortly before 1000 BC was the selection of a monarchy. They chose a king, one who would go before them and fight their battles for them.

The Problem. By the time the book of Samuel ends, the people have made a disappointing discovery. They discovered that no system in itself can take the place of individual responsibility and righteousness: the government without always depends on there being a government within. A monarchy could not create a righteous or a strong nation. That depended finally on the people.

T. S. Eliot looked down into the dark shadows of the world and offered this warning: "Do you think that the Faith has conquered the world and that lions no longer need keepers? Do you need to be told that whatever has been, can still be? . . . (You) constantly try to escape from the darkness outside and within by dreaming of systems so perfect that no one will need to be good. But the man that is will shadow the man that pretends to be. And the Son of Man was not crucified once for all . . . but the Son of Man is always crucified."[3]

There is no system so perfect that we are relieved of the hard duties of integrity and righteousness. Who needs to hear this? A congregation which believes that erecting a brand new sanctuary will bring vitality to a church made up of disinterested and lethargic people. A couple who hope that a new house will give strength to a family falling apart because of selfishness and thoughtlessness. Parents who offer their children things instead of personal example. A nation which hopes that an election will relieve people of personal responsibilities.

Most of us know down deep that a change of externals will not do it, a new year, a new administration, a new suit, a new order of service. We are still the same people inside, deciding with our actions what shall rule our lives. "You belong to the power you choose to obey."

This is our eternal predicament, one which the book of Samuel illustrates over and again. Within that newly adopted system, the old familiar battles of character were taking place. Does David remain faithful to his wife, or does he not? Does Saul obey the laws he himself has established, or does he not? Is Bathsheba fair to all David's children, or is she not? Does Amnon treat Tamar with respect, or does he not? Does Absalom honor his father David, or does he not?

In every case, one choice represents good, and the other evil, and no externally imposed system frees us from that inconvenient fact. There simply is no system so perfect that we do not have to be good, and so the people of Israel discovered.

The Conclusion. Here, then, is a dynamic book that makes no effort to hide the blemishes that mark its people. It tells of their plaintive hopes that a new system of government, a monarchy, will solve their problems. It describes the struggles of that new system under Saul and David, and of the slow realization of the people that they faced the same basic problems they did before. The people discovered that a new system was not the complete answer, and then they continued on their quest, bruised from the experience but determined nonetheless.

It may be that this is where you find yourself right at this moment. You have tried a dozen new approaches to that problem that most vexes you, but it still remains. In your effort to be a child of God, you are still on the path, searching for a system by which to live.

There is but one way! Centuries after David died, the Israelites were to discover that it wasn't a system they needed, but a Savior. That is what God sent, and to those who accept him, then and now, he gives power to become children of God.

5 JOB
A Book of Grace

Frankly, this is not the way I would run the world if I were God, would you? Jesus says right here in Matthew 5:45 that God makes his sun to rise on the evil and on the good, and sends rain on the just and on the unjust. Somehow that seems like a waste of divine power.

If *I* were God, the bad ones and the good ones would be able to tell by what happened to them just where they stood in my sight. For example, do you think I would ever let a deacon playing golf on Sunday morning shoot a 72? Not on your life! I would fix it so that hooks and slices would drive him straight back to church where he belongs, bogeys on Sunday morning, birdies Sunday afternoon.

If *I* were running the world, shriveled gardens and run-down batteries and rheumatism would appear only among the sinners in the community. Complex cloud formations would let the rain fall in neat, checkerboard patterns all over town.

The first Psalm would be my platform. According to this Psalm, the righteous would prosper, but the wicked would be like "chaff which the wind drives away." (Ps. 1:4) It is a known fact that God is all-powerful, and if he has it, he surely ought to use it, if not flaunt it. Let him reward the righteous and punish the wicked, else there is little point in having a God at all!

Nonetheless, here is Jesus saying that God does not operate that way, that he sends his sun and rain on all people equally, whether they are good or bad. Where do you stand on this question? How do you think God runs the world?

This is the question at the heart of the book of Job. How does God run the world? Specifically, the question rose in connection with the problem of suffering. Do people suffer because God is punishing them for some sin? Do they prosper because God is rewarding them for goodness?

It is thought sometimes that Job handles the question, "Why do people suffer?" It would be more accurate to say that the book concerns the question, "Why do *good* people suffer?" The suffering of the evil caused no real theological problem for Job or his generation. Obviously, the evil *deserved* to suffer. But when good people were seen to be subject to the same misfortunes as the evil, there was much uncertainty about the goodness and the justice of God.

The book of Job was written to deal with this question. The book begins with a narrative introduction of two chapters which sets the stage for all that is to follow. Job was a prosperous man with tremendous wealth and a fine family. Satan suggested to God that Job was righteous because he was well paid for his righteousness. "Has not Job good reason to be God-fearing? Have you not hedged him round on every side with your protection, him and his family and all his possessions? . . . But stretch out your hand and touch all that he has, and then he will curse you to your face." (Job 1:9-11 NEB)

So God agreed to a test, and all Job's children, his property, his wealth, and his health were taken from him, in spite of the fact that he had been a good and righteous man. Then came the black night of despair for Job. In his misery, sick and bereaved, he was visited by three friends, Eliphaz, Bildad, and Zophar. (Job 2:11) For seven days and nights, they simply sat with Job in silence, sharing his grief. But then they began to talk, and their sympathy turned to accusation. Most of the remainder of the book is a poetic account of the discussion Job had with his three friends. Each friend made a statement to which Job gave response. Three times the cycle was repeated. Then came a fourth friend, Elihu, who tried to make sense out of the situation. (Job 32-37)

Finally, in chapters 38-41, God himself spoke out of the whirlwind, and although Job's question as to why a righteous man suffers was never specifically answered, the hurt of Job's heart *was* answered. Then, Job was able to accept his predicament with peace. The book's final chapter was added much later by someone who wanted the story to come out happily. In it, Job's fortune and his family were restored, and he lived happily ever after.

Look more closely at the explanation of suffering offered by Job's three friends. Recall that Job was suffering severely, and he yearned to know how a just God could permit a righteous man to suffer unjustly. The three friends could not accept Job's suggestion that God's system of justice might have gone awry. God's books could not be wrong, they suggested, and so their solutions to the problem were simple and assured.

"Job," they said, "you have sinned and God is punishing you. You simply cannot remember your sin, but it is obvious that if you had not sinned, you would not be suffering like this. God does not make mistakes in his bookkeeping, so if you are suffering, you must have sinned."

Let these three friends speak for themselves. Put yourself in Job's place as your hear these arguments. You believe yourself to have been righteous, but you are desperately sick and in real pain. You have lost your fortune and are grieving at the death of all your children. Imagine, in this setting, your friends saying confidently to you that God ". . .pays a man according to his work and sees that he gets what his conduct deserves." (Job 34:11 NEB) ". . .if you are innocent and upright, then indeed will he watch over you and see your just intent fulfilled." (Job 8:6 NEB)

So Job's friends described their position, one very difficult to rebut in argument. I once knew of a father who would ask the little one around his house to go to bed at night by saying, "You need to go to bed. You look tired."

"I'm *not* tired," the little one would answer.

"Good," the father would say, "then before you get tired, you need to go to bed."

Job's friends could say, "Job, you suffer because you have sinned."

"I have *not* sinned," Job's answer would come.

"Aha!" his friends would say, "that's your sin right there, your pride which makes you think you are innocent." It is the "Catch-22" of this discussion of theodicy, the justice of God. You must have sinned, because you are now suffering.

Job's fourth friend, Elihu, arrived late on the scene, with a slightly different idea. Although he agreed basically with the three other friends, Elihu also offered the opinion that pain and suffering were sent by God as a discipline. Suffering grows strength in a person just as exercise grows muscles. "God has sent this suffering," Elihu seemed to say, "so that you can grow stronger as you endure it." "Man learns his lesson on a bed of pain, tormented by a ceaseless ague in his bones. . . ." (Job 33:19 NEB) "Those who suffer he rescues through suffering and teaches them by the discipline of affliction." (Job 36:15 NEB)

So Job sat in the ashes and listened as his friends attempted to justify God's ways with his people.

Here, then, are the different positions, and we who live today in a world of suffering can see those ideas and make our choices from among them.

One position is that God is a giant paymaster, a bookkeeper doling out to people an immediate reward or punishment for their actions, good for good, evil for evil. This may well be a comforting position for a person so long as that person is prosperous and healthy and never knows the dark night of despair.

At first thought, this is the way some of us would manage things were we God. A second thought shows us how difficult it would be to arrange. If a person takes a long automobile trip and interprets the incessant rain along the way as a sign of God's displeasure with him, he must wonder about all the other people along the way who also experience the dreary weather. Is God displeased with *everyone* along the way? How can God arrange a discriminating rain?

Or, assuming that the falling of the rain is a sign of God's blessing as it was in Jesus' statement in Matthew, on whom would we have the rain fall if we were God? Here is a person who votes as we do, but his faith is different. That one goes to the same church we do, but he doesn't give regularly. The other one gives generously, but he votes for the opposition, and so on with everyone. Soon we are apt to be saying that the rain may fall only on us and our son John, and we are not always sure that John does not deserve an occasional dry spell.

How hard it would be for God to have the rain fall only on the righteous. And Jesus said that this simply is not the way God works in the world. Indeed, would we want it that way? Is there any one of us who really wants justice from God? No, it is mercy we need more than justice, isn't it? A placard for sale at a service station was addressed to husbands, and it said, "If your wife doesn't treat you like you deserve, be thankful." One of our greatest blessings is that God does not treat us as we deserve, but rather, with mercy and with love.

Finally in the book comes God's own statement, a statement which by its affirmations and grand descriptions of the natural world makes us say even as we wonder about the problem of suffering, "How great thou art!" As one reads chapters 40 and 41, one gains the feeling that the human mind will never fully understand God's purposes or his methods. Persons who cannot understand, much less duplicate, God's setting of the stars in motion, surely could not understand the problem of suffering in the world.

In reality, God does not discuss Job's problem in his statement. He certainly does not support the claim that Job was suffering because he had sinned. He offers no explanation for the suffering but, in a majestic way, underlines and emphasizes the fact that he has in his hands the whole world of his creation, from the Pleiades in the heavens to the fish in the sea to every human being ever born on this good earth.

And suddenly, it seems that Job was satisfied—not because he had received a clever answer to the eternal problem but satisfied because God cared enough to answer at all. After the voice from the whirlwind had spoken, Job said, "I knew of thee then only by report, but now I see thee with my own eyes. Therefore, I melt away; I repent in dust and ashes." (Job 42:5 NEB) The God who set the stars in their courses answered him, and out of pain Job found faith. We remember Robert Hamilton's words:

I walked a mile with pleasure; she chatted all the way,
But I was none the wiser for what she had to say.
I walked a mile with sorrow, and not a word said she,
But oh, the things I learned from her when sorrow walked with me![1]

How good it is for us to remember as we sit in the ashes sifting through the debris of a life gone bad or as we hear the ominous words of a doctor's bad report, how strengthening it is to remember that God has us in his hands. He has numbered the very hair on our heads and notices when even a sparrow falls to the ground. It is out of the whirlwind of despair that we are most apt to hear God's Word.

And most of all, how releasing and liberating it is for us to be able to reject the old but stubborn notion that God loves us *only if we are good,* that he is the divine Trick-or-Treater giving us candy when we are good and mischief when we are bad.

Job is a book of grace, of undeserved favor. It says what Jesus said—that the rain falls alike on the just and the unjust because God loves them all. After all, his most magnificent gift came not because we deserved it, but because he loved us. "God loved the world so much that he gave his only Son, that everyone who has faith in him may not die but have eternal life. It was not to judge the world that God sent his Son into the world, but that through him the world might be saved." (John 3:16-17 NEB) God sends the rain and the sun, and he sends Jesus Christ for all people, for you, for me, even in our stumbling and our falling.

The next time the rain falls with its gentle touch, and the next time the sun sets in a blaze of glory for all to see, remember that it is for all his children that God's love is given. This is what he assures us in Job, a book of God's grace.

6 THE PSALMS
Mirror to Humanity

Her experience was one through which many of us have gone. "Take this questionnaire into the next room and fill it out," the personnel director said. "Take your time, because we want to know what you're like before deciding on whether to give you the job." The first part of the application form was easy, she discovered: names and dates and places. But the second part dealt with opinions and attitudes, and ended with the instruction to complete this sentence: "The most significant thing about me is. . ." Is what? She got the job, but completing that last sentence was the hardest part of the task.

How would you complete it, right at this moment? "The most significant thing about me is. . ." Is what? The writers of the 150 Psalms in the Old Testament give a variety of answers to that question: "The most significant thing about me is that I am afraid. The most significant thing about me is that I am heartbroken, lonely, guilt-ridden. God, the most significant thing about me is that I am thankful, I am secure in your hands, I believe in your presence."

Notice the uniqueness of the Psalms. They are different from all other books of the Bible. Other books contain God's Word addressed to his people through prophets and historians and evangelists. The Psalms reverse that process: they are words addressed to God by his people. Some would call them prayers. Others would call them hymns. In either case, the book is a window through which we can see deep into the souls of people who pour out their answers to that incomplete sentence: "The most significant thing about me is that. . ." What?

We can get as technical as we desire when discussing the Psalms. We can note that this is the longest book in the Bible and contains 150 chapters. In an obvious imitation of the first five books of the Bible, the Law, this book is divided into five sections, each of which ends with a benediction. We can observe that seventy-three of the Psalms are ascribed to David but that other authors are named. Psalm 90 is ascribed to Moses, Psalms 72 and 127 to Solomon. Two of the Psalms are identical, Psalms 14 and 53, indicating that our present book is likely a compilation of several collections of popular songs or prayers. They range in date from 1000 BC to 350 BC. We recognize that we are reading Hebrew poetry in the Psalms and that even in the original language there is no rhyming. Hebrew poetry depends on meter, not rhyme, for its uniqueness.

There are many technical points about the book that any good commentary describes. These points are all important, but they do not really show us the spirit of the book with its deeply expressed human feelings. A scientist defines a kiss as "a juxtaposition of two orbicular muscles in a state of contraction." While the definition is accurate, most of us know that it does not catch the full dimension of a kiss.

The book of Psalms is a mirror of all that moves us in life. John Calvin called the book "an anatomy of all the parts of the soul." And how different are the seasons of the soul. These differences are found among different people but also within any one of us at different times. The moods of our own soul change so rapidly that within one individual the shadows deepen, then lengthen, then disappear entirely as life moves on. It is a great variety of moods and needs that the Psalms describe.

A church school teacher once asked his class of sixth graders if they could think of anything God couldn't do. "I can," one boy told the startled teacher. "He can't please everybody." And no wonder! How different we are from one another. When we observe the great variety of moods that work themselves into the prayers of the Psalms, we see confirmation of the sixth grader's pronouncement. For example, in a sort of "I'm OK, you're OK" Psalm one writer says: ". . .I have walked in my integrity, and I have trusted in the Lord without wavering. . . . I walk in faithfulness to thee. . . . I wash my hands in innocence. . . ." (Psalm 26:1, 3, 6) Another says, ". . . I will confess my transgressions to the Lord. . . ." (Ps. 32:5) One Psalmist says, ". . .my days pass away like smoke, ... My days are like an evening shadow; . . . ." (Ps. 102:3, 11) The writer in the very next Psalm says that the Lord satisfies him with good and renews his youth like the eagle's. (Ps. 103:5)

Not only do we see varieties of moods in the thoughts of the Psalmists but also some feelings that are considerably less than noble. Here is the prayer of one writer who is speaking of his enemies: "O God, break the teeth in their mouths; tear out the fangs of the young lions. . . . Let them be like the snail which dissolves into slime. . . . The righteous will rejoice when he sees the vengeance; he will bathe his feet in the blood of the wicked." (Psalm 58:6, 8, 10) It is not always a pretty sight when we look down inside our souls, for here is someone who is obviously saying, "The most significant fact about me is that I hate my enemies and want vengeance."

Let us look, then, at what others of the Psalmists show is of greatest significance in their own lives. We will see that the book is a mirror of where we have been at many times in life, perhaps where we are right now. These categories are scattered at random through the book, so that when we start reading it we will quickly come to a passage which will make us say, "That is the way I feel right now."

Many of the Psalm writers say, *"The most significant thing about me is that I am brokenhearted, and I cannot stand my grief."* Consider words such as these: "Save me, O God! For the waters have come up to my neck. I sink in deep mire, where there is no foothold; I have come into deep waters, and the flood sweeps over me. I am weary with my crying; my throat is parched. My eyes grow dim with waiting for my God." (Ps. 69:1-3) "My God, my God, why hast thou forsaken me? Why art thou so far from helping me, from the words of my groaning? O my God, I cry by day, but thou dost not answer; and by night, but find no rest." (Ps. 22:1-2) "I am weary with my moaning; every night I flood my bed with tears; I drench my couch with my weeping. My eye wastes away because of grief; it grows weak because of all my foes." (Ps. 6:6-7)

Who of us has not felt this? At one time or another, the iron enters the souls of all of us and we grieve deeply. Alfred Tennyson describes this condition perfectly:

> But what am I?
> An infant crying in the night:
> An infant crying for the light:
> And with no language but a cry.[1]

"The most significant thing about me is that I am brokenhearted."

A second group of writers say in their Psalms, *"The most significant thing about me is that I am afraid."* Listen to what they say:

"I am poured out like water, and all my bones are out of joint; my heart is like wax, it is melted within my breast; my strength is dried up like a potsherd, and my tongue cleaves to my jaws; thou dost lay me in the dust of death." (Ps. 22:14-15) "Hear my prayer, O Lord; let my cry come to thee! Do not hide thy face from me in the days of my distress! . . . For my days pass away like smoke, and my bones burn like a furnace. My heart is smitten like grass, and withered. . . ." (Ps. 102:1-3) "Give ear to my prayer, O God; and hide not thyself from my supplication! Attend to me, and answer me; I am overcome by my trouble. . . . Fear and trembling come upon me, and horror overwhelms me. And I say, 'O that I had wings like a dove! I would fly away and be at rest. . . .' " (Ps. 55:1-2, 5-6)

"The most significant thing about me? I am afraid!"

Another group of writers say, *"The most significant thing about me is that I am lonely."* "Turn thou to me, and be gracious to me; for I am lonely and afflicted." (Ps. 25:16)

All of us have had such feelings, but some among us are especially vulnerable to the ache of loneliness. Anyone who has visited a nursing home for older persons has heard, almost verbatim, words such as these: "I cry aloud to God, . . . that he may hear me. . . . Thou dost hold my eyelids from closing; I am so troubled that I cannot speak. I consider the days of old, I remember the years long ago. I commune with my heart in the night. . . ." (Ps. 77:1, 4-7) "My friends and companions stand aloof from my plague, and my kinsmen stand afar off." (Ps. 38:11) "I am . . . a horror to my neighbors, an object of dread to my acquaintances; those who see me in the street flee from me. I have passed out of mind like one who is dead; I have become like a broken vessel." (Ps. 31:11-12)

"The most significant thing about me is that I am lonely!"

But we have started with the dark side of the moon, and perhaps one would feel by now that the whole book is the voice of the infant crying in the night—sorrow and grief and loneliness. These elements are frequent, to be sure, for it was a hard life these people led. But other voices are there, too. Many of the writers say with joy, *"The most significant fact about me is that I am forgiven!"*

"The Lord is merciful and gracious, slow to anger and abounding in steadfast love . . . . as far as the east is from the west, so far does he remove our transgressions from us. As a father pities his children, so the Lord pities those who fear him." (Ps. 103:8, 12-13) "If thou, O Lord, shouldst mark iniquities, Lord, who could stand? But there is forgiveness with thee. . . ." (Ps. 130:3-4)

"The most significant thing about me is that I am forgiven!"

Other writers say, *"The most significant thing about me is that I am grateful for this abundance I have been given.*" "It is good to give thanks to the Lord, to sing praises to thy name, O Most High; to declare thy steadfast love in the morning, and thy faithfulness by night." (Ps. 92:1-2) "I waited patiently for the Lord; he inclined to me and heard my cry. He drew me up from the desolate pit, out of the miry bog, and set my feet upon a rock. . . . He put a new song in my mouth, a song of praise to our God." (Ps. 40:1-3)

Here is a classic statement that seems tailor-made for thanksgiving. A more beautiful expression of the benevolence and nurture of God would be hard to find: "Thou visitest the earth and waterest it, thou greatly enrichest it; the river of God is full of water; thou providest their grain, for so thou hast prepared it. Thou waterest its furrows abundantly, settling its ridges, softening it with showers and blessing its growth. . . . The pastures of the wilderness drip, the hills gird themselves with joy, the meadows clothe themselves with flocks, the valleys deck themselves with grain, they shout and sing together for joy." (Ps. 65:9, 10, 12)

"I am grateful, Lord, for all this you have given!"

We hear one last group saying, *"The most significant fact about me is that I trust in God,"* and some of the best known of the Psalms say this. We know best the beautiful Psalm of the Good Shepherd, Psalm 23, but there are others of great beauty as well. "He who dwells in the shelter of the Most High, who abides in the shadow of the Almighty, will say to the Lord, . . . 'my God, in whom I trust.' . . . he will cover you with his pinions, and under his wings you will find refuge. . . ." (Ps. 91:1-3) "In peace I will both lie down and sleep; for thou alone, O Lord, makest me dwell in safety." (Ps. 4:8)

"The Lord is my light and my salvation; whom shall I fear? The Lord is the stronghold of my life; of whom shall I be afraid?" (Ps. 27:1) "Lord, thou hast been our dwelling place in all generations. Before the mountains were brought forth, or ever thou hadst formed the earth and the world, from everlasting to everlasting thou art God." (Ps. 90:1-2)

"The most significant thing about me is that I trust in God, and I live and die in his hands."

There are many others, of course, but these suffice to show what a range of experiences and emotions is covered by these voices from the Psalms. It is little wonder that both at the joy of his baptism and the anguish of his crucifixion it was the Psalms that Jesus called to mind. (Ps.

2:7 and 22:1) He knew them well. He knew their assertions of truth and faith, knew their eloquent cries of sorrow, and knew all the ranges of emotion in between. Some of the books of the Bible speak of where we ought to be in faith, but the Psalms, without apology or hesitation, speak of where we are. We find in this book thoughts that describe every human condition and bring God close at hand.

People in the West have a legend about a taciturn old cowboy who was never one for praying eloquent prayers but who had a copy of the Lord's Prayer on the wall by his bed. Each night before retiring he would, in a small moment of devotion, nod his head at the prayer on the wall and say, "Lord, them's my sentiments." It may be, with the Psalms, that this is the best some of us can do in our expression of faith. There come times when the hurt is too deep, the fear too great, the joy too unbounded for us to find words sufficient to the occasion. Paul once said, ". . .we do not know how to pray as we ought, but the Spirit himself intercedes for us with sighs too deep for words." (Romans 8:26)

When in our lives there come experiences that call forth emotions too deep for our words, we can look quickly to the Psalms and stand on the shoulders of those who have already said it for us. Whether in grief or in joy, whether in fear or in faith, whether in anxiety or in assurance, if we turn to the Psalms and let their message fill our lives, we will be given the ability to say through it all, "O Lord, our Lord, how majestic is thy name in all the earth!" (Ps. 8:1)

7 PROVERBS
On Using Your Head

There are 613 laws in the Old Testament, 613 specific commandments and prohibitions, and one would think that these 613 laws should cover almost everything a person could think of doing. Any parent, of course, knows that they could not. Parents go out for an evening, leaving the children at home, and as they leave, they review the rules. Don't go outdoors. Don't open the door if someone knocks. Don't try to light the fireplace. The parents continue the list as long as time permits. On returning home a few hours later, the parents learn that they did not think to say, "Don't make pancakes and eat them in the living room," and that is exactly what the children did. "You didn't say not to!" Laws cannot cover every conceivable situation, and so the wise parent is apt to emphasize, "Use your head! Use your common sense," and hope that things like pancakes in the living room will be ruled out.

There are five books of Law in the Old Testament that contain 613 specific injunctions, but there is one book that tries to say what the wise parent says: "Use your head. Use common sense." "My son," says Proverbs, "keep sound wisdom and discretion. . .and they will be life for your soul. . . ." (Prov. 3:21, 22)

Here is a book that brings life by reminding its readers of the daily need for common sense in the living out of life. It contains no laws, no history, no prophetic sermons. It is, along with Job and Ecclesiastes, referred to as one of the "Books of Wisdom" in the Old Testament.

Who wrote it? One could almost as easily ask, "Who wrote *Bartlett's Quotations?*" Many people wrote it. Solomon was famed for his wisdom and surely wrote a number of the proverbs in the book as the introductory verses indicate. (Prov. 1:1, 25:1) But other authors are named as well. Some proverbs were credited to a man named Agur (Prov. 30:1) and others to Lemuel (Prov. 31:1). In its present form, the book is an anthology of Hebrew wise sayings collected over many pre-Christian centuries. It says little about worship, nothing about Israel's grand history, nothing about immortality or resurrection. It is a book which seeks to offer common sense advice on how to live here and now in a difficult world.

The reader can open this book to any page and be delighted with its witty advice. It is written largely from the male point of view, as might be suspected if a person like Solomon is the author of portions of it. There are frequent references to problems men have with their wives. ". . .a nagging wife is like water dripping endlessly," one proverb says. (Prov. 19:13 NEB) "Better to live alone in the desert than with a nagging and ill-tempered wife." (Prov. 21:19 NEB) "Like a gold ring in a pig's snout is a beautiful woman without good sense." (Prov. 11:22 NEB) It should not be surprising to learn from I Kings 11:3 that Solomon had seven hundred wives! There are no references whatever to cranky and stubborn husbands in the book.

Anyone who does not like to read or hear references to the intimacies of life at home had best stay away from Proverbs. It speaks candidly of daily life at home. "Better a dish of vegetables if love go with it than a fat ox eaten in hatred." (Prov. 15:17 NEB) "A soft answer turns away anger, but a sharp word makes tempers hot." (Prov. 15:1 NEB)

Hundreds of such proverbs are found in the book, and many of them will speak directly and sharply to the reader. But through all of them, there runs this central thread of thought: God has given you a mind, so use it! Common sense is essential to the good life.

This is one obvious message the book brings to us in the church today: *many of our problems can be solved by using common sense.* We need that message, for even in our relationship with our church and our obligations connected with it, common sense is often far away.

Here is a father and mother who will go to extraordinary lengths to give their children an education. They will drive the child to music lessons and encourage practice. They will see that their child is in school regularly. They would never think of saying about school, "The children don't really want to go, and so I just say, 'Why make them?' " But in the matter of that same child's religious education, her training in moral and ethical values, her learning the discipline of regular worship, it is a different approach entirely.

Here is a fellow who attends a civic club regularly. If he is absent, he makes up a meeting at some other club. Every week without fail he arranges his schedule so that he can meet and eat and listen. Ten years of perfect attendance, he says proudly. "Listen," he says, "I would like to go to church, but there just isn't time. Too busy, you know. Too many other commitments." He expects his religion to get him to heaven, but it won't even get him to church on Sunday! What he needs is a touch of common sense, of reason, of honesty.

Here is a family that has every good thing going for them, new car, fine house, every material gift imaginable. There is always money to be spent when occasions arise. But every year when the church asks for some kind of financial commitment for the year ahead, they return bleak looks and the excuse of hard times. Common sense is needed to help us compare what we have with what we give.

The book of Proverbs says to us that we don't need miracles in daily life as much as we need common sense and discipline. God gave us minds to use so that we might know the truth, and it is startling that we use those minds as little as we do.

But the book points beyond this to a larger truth: *reason is one of God's grandest gifts to his people.* It is a doorway to God. This book testifies to the sacredness of reason, and reminds us of Jesus' teaching: "You shall love the Lord your God with all your. . .mind!" (Matthew 22:37)

Such a view is not always accepted. There are those who feel that reason is an enemy of faith and religion. Halford Luccock puts it like this: "Moslems, on entering a mosque, remove their shoes and leave them outside; Christians, all too often, entering the church, remove their brains and leave them outside."[1] Church, it is said, is a place for believing, not for thinking. It is a place for the soul, not the mind. Religion is a matter of commitment, not of intelligence.

This approach shows up frequently in our attitudes about study of the Bible. We often grow suspicious of those who point out that the Bible was written in three different languages over a dozen centuries, who study and analyze the oldest manuscripts we have of God's Word, who try to determine the marvelous historical process it has gone through to get to us today. No place for critical thought in the study of scripture, it is said. If you love the Bible, you leave your brain outside and accept it uncritically. Reason and thought are out of place.

There's no place for reason in prayer, some would say. It is all a matter of spirit, and reason has no place here. Yet Paul says in Corinthians, ". . .I will pray with the spirit, and I will pray with the mind also." (I Cor. 14:15) J. Edgar Park tells this story: "During the blitz in World War II an old woman in London had escaped, while all the lower part of her street had been demolished with much loss of life. The rector called next morning, and she said, 'I never prayed so hard in my life as I did last night. Every bomb I heard coming I prayed hard and pushed it farther down the street. I can never thank God enough.' The rector said, 'Yes, but wasn't it rather hard on the folk who live at the other end of your street?' She said, 'Oh, they should have prayed as hard as I did and pushed it right out into the sea.' "[2]

Thought and reason are as appropriate in prayer as anywhere at all. There is need to pray with the mind as well as the spirit for the mind is the surest doorway to God. Even the spirit that fills us is subject to be run through the filter of our minds. John says, "Beloved, do not believe every spirit, but test the spirits to see whether they are of God. . . ." (I John 4:1) Use your minds!

Why is it that some very religious people are so suspicious of reason? Why do some feel that the scientists and philosophers are dangerous to Christian faith? Is our faith in God so fragile that we think a scientist's discovery of a new truth can destroy it? Is God that small?

Is the truth contained in the Bible, for example, so fragile that a scholar studying the texts and manuscripts of the Bible can destroy it? Surely not! We ought to use every ability of reason we have to study that ancient book, study its languages, its varied texts, its curious transmission through the centuries. No fact about the Bible which is true can ever hurt it for God *is* truth.

Are we really afraid that old Dr. Leakey and his kin, out digging with pick and shovel in the rocky canyons of East Africa, will discover something that will discredit God, who created it all? Our little systems might get shaken, yes. Our own ideas might get overturned, to be sure. But is our God so fragile that the chance turning over of a crusty, ancient bone will destroy him? Surely not! Everything we discover about the amazing story of how God created this universe adds to the wonder of it.

Do we really think that if we continue to meddle out there in the cold distances of space we might discover something that will bring God like a falling star to our feet? Surely we will not. The heavens declare the glory of God, and the wider and the more amazing the heavens turn out to be, the wider and more amazing becomes the creative force behind it all. Proverbs puts it this way: "The Lord, by wisdom, founded the earth; by understanding he established the heavens; by his knowledge the deeps broke forth, and the clouds drop down the dew." (Prov. 3:19-20)

The mind of the scientist is continually at work probing this universe unceasingly. Even now, the great radio-telescopes at Caguas in Puerto Rico listen to distant galaxies, the space capsules with their sensitive eyes circle distant planets, the astronomers look out to the edge of space and time. And looking inward all this time are the geneticists and the microbiologists and the psychiatrists and philosophers, and all are seeking truth which is the essence of God himself.

Our little systems may bend and sway as new truth comes, but the fact of God's creation can only find new evidence as the human mind reaches outward. Every time the modern scientific mind uncovers another incredible fact about this universe, we know that much more about God. Science and religion and philosophy are all channels flowing toward the reality of God, and one day they will all flow together for the object of them all is truth, one of God's other names.

Ah, but now comes the final objection. If wisdom and reason are so exalted, why the need for Christ? Why cannot men and women through their reason know God completely?

It is clear that wisdom and reason are never quite enough. If they exist by themselves, something is missing. A farmer from the Midwest once put an ad in the paper: "I am fifty-eight years old. Would like to marry a young woman of thirty who has a tractor. Please send a picture of the tractor." Certainly, knowledge and reason are present in the farmer's strategy, but something is missing from the story. Knowledge and reason are inadequate.

Remember how Paul put it? ". . .as for prophecies, they will pass away; as for tongues, they will cease; as for knowledge, it will pass away." (I Cor. 13:8) All of these are of value, but they pass away, and what is finally left is love. Reason and knowledge can never really understand the dimension of love, and this is why they alone are not enough. Can any of us explain rationally why our spouse loves us? Love is the one dimension that reason can never explain, and Christ came in human form so that we might see living proof of the basic fact of all, that God *is* love.

And this is why Proverbs is not the final book of the Bible. "The Queen of the South . . . came from the ends of the earth to hear the wisdom of Solomon, and behold, *something greater than Solomon is here.*" (Luke 11:31 [Italics added]) Something greater than wisdom! Wisdom takes us a step beyond law, to be sure, but it stops a step short of love. Then with the most ancient books we say, "Learn God's law, and obey it," and with Proverbs we say, "Seek wisdom, and live it." But we complete the picture by adding, "The love of God is seen in Christ Jesus. Accept him as the Lord of your life."

8 JEREMIAH
On Being Negative

"Surely this is the worst generation God has permitted to exist on this earth! Just look at us—what a shoddy level of commitment we show, here at church, here in this city we brag about, and especially in this nation. How long do we think God will let us exist like this? We're faithless people living in a sinful world, and it doesn't seem to bother us a bit!"

If Jeremiah were here, that's the way he probably would begin his sermon, because there just wasn't much in this world with which Jeremiah was satisfied. *Nothing* measured up, and Jeremiah attacked it all. He condemned his own townspeople (11:21), the false prophets of his day (23:9-40), the priests in the temple (20:1), the rulers of the land (36:19), the military authorities (38:4). He was a champion negative thinker and was remembered for that. Indeed, later generations took his name, Jeremiah, and made a new word of it—"jeremiad." It's in the dictionary, defined as "a lamenting and denunciatory complaint." (Parenthetically, it's interesting, or sobering, to wonder what meaning would be given to *my* name, or *yours,* if people should make a noun out of it!) Jeremiah's name became synonymous with complaint and criticism. Day and night and day, lashing out at the world about him, he was a champion negative thinker.

You find his long prophetic book in the Old Testament. He lived about 600 years before Christ in a particularly critical period in Israel's history. All the dreams about Israel were tumbling down. Babylon was looming on the eastern horizon, and Jeremiah watched as his own little nation weakened and died. Then, it was carried away into captivity in the year 586 BC with Jerusalem and its temple utterly destroyed. In short, he had much to be negative about! The message of the book shines through the life of the man and illuminates both the weaknesses and the strengths of negativism.

Start, then, by noting *how easy it is to get into this pattern of negativism.* It requires no skills whatsoever. Once each year many of us who could not run nonstop from one end zone to the other will sit and find fault with a Super Bowl player who drops a ball. Many of us who never even take the trouble to vote still find time to condemn those who serve in elective office. We can't write books, but we can deride them. We can't play an instrument, but we can tell the world what we don't like about how someone else does.

Negative thinking can expand to deal with theories about how the universe began, or it can contract to cover the typographical error in the worship bulletin. It can range from the proper response to the Polish crisis to the shape of Barbra Streisand's nose, from the food shortage in Biafra to what we had for supper last night. Negative thinking—a modern problem!

Why are we so negative? There are different reasons, no doubt, but we surely share with Jeremiah one characteristic that makes criticism so frequent—Jeremiah didn't particularly like himself! When God first called him to speak up, Jeremiah was negative *about himself.* He couldn't do it! "Ah, Lord God!" said Jeremiah. "Behold, I do not know how to speak, for I am only a youth." (1:6)

Anyone who is negative about himself or herself is almost inevitably going to be negative about the family, the community, the church, the world. Time after time it has been clinically proven: deal with a person's unspoken complaints against himself and you will have satisfied most of his complaints against his world. Trying to make the negative thinker happy by correcting the "typo" in the worship bulletin or improving the menu for supper is like treating a headache with a haircut. That's not really the problem. Part of the explanation for our negative thinking is that we don't always like ourselves, and so we don't like anything else either.

And frankly, some people find such negativism fun and exhilarating. Strangely, most of us respond with more interest to a harshly negative sermon than we do to a gently positive one. When the sermon includes a lambasting of our society and points out how bad things are, we always get many requests for sermon copies from our radio listeners, far more than when some milder subject is covered. It is more interesting to listen to, and it is stimulating to preach, too. There's something satisfying about "pointing out the trouble" from a thoroughly professional vantage point. Two taxidermists once stopped before a store window in which an owl was on display. They immediately began to criticize the way it was mounted. Its eyes were not natural, its wing was not in proportion with its head, its feathers were not neatly arranged, and its feet could certainly be improved. When they had finished their criticism, the old owl there in the pet store window turned his head and winked at them!

Whether it was because of his own insecurity, or because it was exhilarating, Jeremiah specialized in negative thinking and probably would have been surprised to know how thoroughly this habit had permeated his life. Would *we* be surprised if we knew how much of our own life was given over to complaint?

A national sportscaster told of his frustrations when some listeners shared their feeling that he was too negative in his comments during telecasts of certain games. Surely he wasn't guilty of this, he thought. In order to test it out, he arranged for an office stenographer to take down every word he uttered at the next event he covered and was abashed to discover how frequently he was, indeed, unnecessarily critical.

Most of us would be startled to read, at the end of a typical day, a script of all we had said during the fourteen hours just ending. We would be surprised at the infrequency of affirmations shared with those we love most. We would be embarassed at how negative we have been from early morn until bedtime. Does a set of comments such as these sound familiar? "Can't those kids ever get out of bed without my shouting at them? This bacon isn't worth cooking, is it? Can't you find your books without my help? How many days in a row have you worn that shirt? Don't slam that door so hard! I told you I would be home as soon as I can—quit nagging me. What a lousy day this was; the traffic was unbelievable. The car is acting up again—didn't you take it to the garage? Spaghetti again for dinner? Why won't those kids do their homework? Look at that! Three runs in the ninth, and we've lost again. Doesn't that manager ever know when to change pitchers? It's eleven o'clock—can't those kids ever go to bed without my shouting at them?"

And so life takes on a cast, a color, and without our knowing it, we are specialists in criticism and fault-finding. Edna St. Vincent Millay's magnificent poem "Renascence" concludes with this jarring observation:

The world stands out on either side
No wider than the heart is wide;
Above the world is stretched the sky
No higher than the soul is high.

The heart can push the sea and land
Farther away on either hand;
The soul can split the sky in two
And let the face of God shine through.
But East and West will pinch the heart
That cannot keep them pushed apart;
And he whose soul is flat—the sky
Will cave in on him by and by.[1]

And yet, having said all this, *sometimes negativism is the only proper response to the realities of the world about us.* When we put Jeremiah in his historical setting and see the crisis his nation was facing, the blindness of its leaders, and the apathy of its people, we do not wonder that Jeremiah was negative! He could not have been a prophet of God and been positive in those days. Someone might easily make the case that one of the weaknesses of our own day is that we are not negative enough about the great issues that face our nation.

Indeed, most of us consider the subjects that Jeremiah dealt with to be off-limits to preachers of today. Jeremiah dealt with political issues in most of his preaching. He dealt with foreign policy: should little Israel ally herself with Egypt or with Babylon? Should Israel depend on increased armaments for her survival, or on God? Those were Jeremiah's sermon topics! But most people today who want their preachers preaching like prophets don't want their preachers preaching about what the prophets preached about!

Then it may well be that at least with regard to national and international problems, we aren't nearly critical enough in this day! With the threat of a nuclear war that would probably kill 100 million Americans in the first two hours, where are our cries for nuclear disarmament? Jeremiah excoriated the preachers of his own day who, as he put it, "healed the wound of my people lightly, saying, 'Peace, peace,' when there is no peace." (6:14) When God sent a prophet in that critical day, he sent him bearing a hard, negative message. Then it may well be that if God weighed the church and its people in the balance today, he would not find us too negative! *He would find us not negative enough about those issues that have always raised the prophetic voice*—about a blind dependence on arms instead of on righteousness, about our callousness toward the poor, our blindness toward those who suffer injustice and discrimination. "What are you saying about this?" God might well ask us. Where is your complaint?

Remember that story about Thoreau, stuck in jail because of some crusade he was on? A friend came visiting and asked, "What are you doing in jail?" And Thoreau quickly responded, "What are you doing *out* of jail?" How do we justify *not* speaking up with a louder voice in view of the aching injuries this world of ours endures? If Jeremiah was negative, he was negative at the right time on the right issues in the right way.

And listen to this! We may remember Jeremiah for his negativism, *but when Jesus began his ministry in Galilee, the people there thought it was Jeremiah come back again.* "Who do people say that I am?" Jesus asked his disciples. "They say that you must be Jeremiah, back from the dead," they answered (Mt. 16:14 Paraphrase). Jesus reminded them of Jeremiah!

This was not because of his joy in finding fault with others but because of the quality of his complaint. Much of *our* criticism is born of bitterness, and every word of it spews out hatred and despair. The negativism of both Jeremiah and Jesus was of a special kind, one which did not rejoice in evil, but grieved at it and offered hope and assurance in God's love. No wonder they thought of Jeremiah when they saw Jesus. There was Jeremiah, looking at weak and stumbling Jerusalem and saying, "Oh that my head were waters, and my eyes a fountain of tears, that I might weep day and night for the slain . . . of my people." (Jer. 9:1) And there is Jesus, weeping over Jerusalem and saying, "Oh Jerusalem, Jerusalem, killing the prophets and stoning those who are sent to you! How often would I have gathered your children together as a hen gathers her brood under her wings, and you would not!" (Mt. 23:37)

Our mistake today is not that we are negative but that we are negative about the wrong things. We are sensitive to personal slights but insensitive to the injustices whole classes of people face. We grow angry when something interferes with personal pleasures but are apathetic before the knowledge that 5,000 people in this world die of starvation every day. We grow alarmed when we see too much violence on television, but we acquiesce continually to an arms buildup so colossal as to destroy the world.

Then for each of us, the problem of negativism is a complicated one as it was for Jeremiah. When is negativism appropriate? Ecclesiastes says there is ". . .a time to break down and a time to build up; a time to weep, and a time to laugh, a time to mourn, and a time to dance. . . ." (Eccl. 3:3-4) How do we know which is which? That is our hard calling, to know when the heart should hold steady and when it should break before the sins of this world. It is good for us to remember that when confronted with the full dimension of human sin both the strong prophet Jeremiah and the strong savior Jesus wept over Jerusalem. We who seldom grow negative about the sins of this world may learn from them.

Writing years ago in the Saturday Review, John Ciardi told of the influx of synthetic emeralds that had flooded the market. So perfect were the synthetics, an expert told him, that there was only one way to tell them from the real thing. If you want to know which of two emeralds is synthetic and which is genuine, heat both stones to a prescribed temperature and give them both a tap with a small hammer. *The one that breaks is the real one.*

Oh God, along with steadfast souls, give us breakable hearts. Amen.

9 AMOS
The Unpopular Preacher

When a preacher gets fired from his job on the very first day of work, it takes no personnel expert to determine that something went wrong. The delicate relationship between pastor and people is indeed a fragile one and is easily upset. A perfect match is rare. The frustrated chairman of a pulpit committee, after having spent several months unsuccessfully searching for a preacher, said, "Those preachers the congregation can stand can't stand the congregation." Still and all, leaving after only one day *is* unusual.

This preacher's dismissal came immediately after the people heard him deliver his first sermon. They chose not to sample a second, and this fact reveals part of the problem. Obviously, he said something which the people did not enjoy hearing. They made the parting quick and clean, and before the boxes had been unpacked or the pictures hung, out went the preacher.

His name was Amos, and the short book which bears his name in the Old Testament includes much of his sermon and a bit of his story. Lest you feel that this is a bit of dry and dusty Hebrew history, unrelated to our present day, let me remind you that although the story, on its surface, involves a Hebrew prophet and his unpopular sermon, the deeper story involves what happens in any age when men and women hear from God a message which does not please them.

It was about 750 BC that the story happened. In order to have a scaffold to hang this date on, recall that it was about a thousand years earlier, around 1750 BC, that Abraham had lived. Moses led Israel out of Egypt about 1250 BC, and David had begun as Israel's first strong king in 1000 BC. That strong nation soon was divided between the northern and southern kingdoms, Israel and Judah, and constant bickering went on between the two halves of the Jewish nation.

About 750 BC, a farmer who lived south of Jerusalem in Tekoa felt the call to preach. A message from God was burning in his bones, and it needed saying. Strangely, it was not to his own people in Judah that Amos was sent, but to the people of the northern kingdom, Israel. The capital city was Bethel, and there on the town square, Amos delivered his first, last, and to our knowledge, only sermon.

We do not know how it happened that someone remembered and put in written form what Amos said at Bethel. Perhaps Amos himself did it, or perhaps it was one of his followers. In any event, Amos was the first of the prophets whose teachings were included in a book bearing his name. What were those teachings? This was a time of international crisis, and Amos quickly got into politics in his message. The giant nation of Assyria was looking over tiny Israel's shoulder, threatening at any time to invade and destroy her. Amos saw the threat of Assyrian invasion as God's punishment for Israel's disobedience and immorality. Israel was rotten through and through, he said. Injustice was everywhere. The poor were exploited by the rich and the courts were corrupt. God's patience with Israel was fast running out, and unless there was complete and immediate repentence, God would unchain his servant, Assyria, and down would come the nation of Israel.

It was in this sense that Amos was a prophet. Today, that word most frequently connotes one who predicts the future. The biblical prophets predicted the future only in the sense of saying that if a nation was not righteous, it would inevitably suffer the consequences. Literally, the word "prophet" means "one who speaks for." Amos, and other Old Testament prophets, were not soothsayers but spokesmen for God. Speaking for God, Amos preached his sermon and was invited to leave Bethel and not come back. He was the unpopular preacher.

Against this background we are moved to ask why it went wrong for Amos. Here was a man of God telling God's people what God wanted them to hear. Yet they asked him to leave. Why? As we seek answers in Amos' time, it would be helpful to decide whether or not we have changed very much in the way *we* respond to prophetic statements of right and wrong that come to us from God today.

The first clue to explain Amos' short ministry in Bethel is this: *as long as he spoke to the people of Bethel about other people's sins, he was on safe ground.* Indeed, this is the way Amos began his sermon. A natural psychologist in his strategy, Amos began by listing and condemning the sins of Israel's hated neighbors. "Woe to Syria," he said, and as he listed Syria's sins, the people nodded in agreement. "Woe to Edom," he said, and the people almost applauded. "Woe to Moab, woe to Amnon. Isn't Phoenicia awful?" Amos even struck out at the southern kingdom, Judah, saying that God would destroy her if she did not change her ways.

It is easy to imagine the reaction of the people of Israel as they heard this fiery prophet from Tekoa condemning all the people they did not like. This man knows what he's talking about, they must have thought. If shouting "Amen!" was customary in that day, the amens would have been shouted for Amos was saying exactly what they wanted to hear. But then, in an abrupt shift, Amos changed targets. "Thus says the Lord: For three transgressions of Israel, and for four, I will not revoke the punishment; because they sell the righteous for silver, and the needy for a pair of shoes—they that trample the head of the poor into the dust of the earth. . . ." (Amos 2:6-7) And here's where Amos lost his congregation.

As long as he discussed the sins of other people, it was a rousing response he got from the people of Israel. But when he began to get personal and meddlesome about the sins of the people to whom he was speaking, the ride was over and the ministry ended. The people were willing to listen to any sermon that did not sting a bit. They wanted a comfortable religion. I remember well my grandfather's medical philosophy which he shared with any youngster who came limping in with an injury. Inevitably, he would pull out a jar of raw turpentine, and unless the grandchild was unusually agile, Granddad would pour that mixture onto the wound. As we would howl in protest, he would voice the old adage that had the weight of Scripture for him, "If it's not stinging, it's not doing any good. A medicine that doesn't sting, doesn't heal."

The same case might be made for the messages of God that preachers today deliver. The tendency is to make the sermon all balm in Gilead. It is considerably safer and much more pleasant to comfort the afflicted than it is to afflict the comfortable. All of us are more willing to listen to a discussion of other people's problems than we are our own. Let a church call a community meeting on drug problems among teenagers, and the room will be packed. Should we call such a meeting to discuss immorality among adults, the minister's office would probably accommodate the crowd that would come.

Amos was the first preacher to make this discovery. If he limits his remarks to the sins of people outside his congregation, he will encounter little trouble. Surely this is why one after another preacher of past years delivered fiery sermons against drinking and dancing to congregations of people who for the most part did neither. Tending the little fences carefully, he ignored the big ones and kept silent about the sins of self-righteousness and hypocrisy.

Learning the wrong lesson from Amos, the overcautious preacher of today will carefully avoid topics that would anger certain people in his or her congregation. This man doesn't like to hear about racism, that one hates the National Council. This woman is weary of sermons about giving, and that one is tired of hearing about the dangers of nuclear war. The larger the congregation, the fewer safe subjects there are, and if the preacher plays this game, he or she is in trouble. Sermon topics are apt to be limited to "Pottery Making in the Bible," or "Cities Paul Visited," or if the preacher is really courageous, "Segregation in South Africa."

As long as Amos spoke about other people's sins, his congregation listened. But when he focused in on their own, the pulpit committee knew that it was back to work again, for Amos was out.

Amos quickly developed step number two for a short ministry. He might conceivably have gotten by with a discussion of respectable and easily managed sins. Surely the people would have tolerated his strongest words about the nature of God, or signs of the end of the world. *But Amos not only talked about their sins, he talked about their worst sins, about injustice and corruption and exploitation of the poor.*

Phyllis McGinley offers a job description for a safe, long-term ministry in her tribute to a certain D. Harcourt:

> The Reverend D. Harcourt, folk agree,
> Nodding their heads in solid satisfaction,
> Is just the man for this community.
> Smart, suave, urbane, but capable of action.
> He pleases where he serves; he marshalls out
> The younger crowd, lacks trace of clerical unction,
> Cheers the Kiwanis and the Eagle Scout,
> Is popular at every social function.
> And in the pulpit eloquently speaks
> On diverse matters with both wit and clarity:
> Art, education, God, the early Greeks,
> Vestry repairs that shortly must begin—
> All things but sin. He seldom mentions sin.[1]

Amos mentioned sin and grew very specific. There was no mistaking the meaning of his words, most of which dealt with economic injustices among the people of Israel: You oppress the poor and crush the needy. You trample on the poor and take from him exactions of wheat. You afflict the righteous, you take bribes, you afflict the needy in the gate. You trample upon the needy and bring the poor of the land to an end, saying, "When will the new moon be over. . .that we may buy the poor for silver and the needy for a pair of sandals and sell the refuse of the wheat?" (Amos 4:1; 5:11-12; 8:4, 6 Paraphrase)

Does it become clearer why Amos' ministry in Bethel was short? The best summary of his words come in that classic prophetic statement of what was really important in religion: "I hate, I despise your feasts and I take no delight in your solemn assemblies. . . . Take away from me the noise of your songs; to the melody of your harps I will not listen. But let justice roll down like waters, and righteousness like an everflowing stream." (5:21, 23-24) And in faint echo nearly 800 years later, we hear Jesus saying, "But woe to you Pharisees! for you tithe mint and rue and every herb, and neglect justice and the love of God." (Luke 11:42)

No wonder Amos was dismissed so quickly! He spoke to the ruling classes of Israel about the very issues they chose to ignore. If staying out of trouble is the first consideration of the prophet or the preacher, he or she should strive to offer sermons as irrelevant as possible to the aching needs of today's world. No one will be offended or inspired, and because boredom works more slowly than anger, ministries will be longer and ministers milder.

As the light of God's word shines through this ancient prophet's words and focuses on our lives today, we confess that there are certain subjects we would prefer that the preacher leave in the study. We are weary of them and we want to hear no more about them. But do we not occasionally get the feeling that the subjects which make us most uncomfortable are probably the ones we need most to confront? Perhaps we have grown tired of hearing about the threat of nuclear war, or the stubborn taint of racism, or the importance of giving, of evangelism, of faithfulness in marriage. It could be that those are the very areas where we are weakest, and it's a natural defense mechanism to want to tune them out.

Have you ever had that experience of relaxing at home when the doorbell unexpectedly rings? Probably you will quickly run to close a closet or bedroom door. Then, with unkempt areas screened off behind closed doors, the visitor is greeted and welcomed in. We join with the ancient people of Bethel in having some rooms and closets and corners of our lives we simply don't want God looking into. There are some subjects we don't want to hear discussed, some words we don't want to hear. As we read from the works of Amos and his kin, we discover that they did not select their topics based on what the people wanted to hear but on the basis of what God wanted said. And more often than not, they had very short ministries.

Amos went back to Tekoa, but the issues he raised remained right there among the people. From this fiery old prophet comes an accurate barometer of our own spiritual health. Which topics do we want let alone? Which messages from God offend us most mightily? *Could it be that the topics that stir us most and make us the angriest are the very ones God is directing straight our way?* And if that is so, what do we intend to do about the hard messages that keep coming today from God's unpopular preachers?

10 THE GOSPEL OF JOHN
Light Shining in the Darkness

"Stop me if you've heard this one," the fellow says. But who ever has the nerve to stop him and say, "Yes, I have heard that story many times before"? Our timidity quickly punishes us as we endure the same story told yet again.

John might have begun his gospel by saying the same thing, because the story of Jesus had already been told, and told very well, three times over. First, Mark had written a simple story of Jesus' life. Then Matthew had written another version of the story, one addressed primarily to Jewish Christians and asserting that Jesus was the long-sought Messiah. In these two gospels, Luke apparently missed sufficient emphasis on the love and compassion of Jesus, so he wrote the story a third time and included material from a different source or two, items that helped him picture Jesus as the gentle friend of the poor and downtrodden.

The "Good News," or "Gospel," had already been told three times. Why did John, much later, feel the need to write yet another story of the life of Jesus? Does he add anything new that helps us on our journey of faith?

A quick reading through the fourth gospel reveals that it is, indeed, quite different from its three precursors. We look in vain at Christmastime for the story of Jesus' birth in John's gospel. It is simply not there. Nor is the story of Jesus' baptism or his temptation found in this book. The Last Supper is not found in John, nor the story of the ascension of Jesus. Most startling of all, we will not find a single parable of Jesus when we read through this book. He may have taught them in parables, as the Scripture says, but John included none of these, not the prodigal son or the good Samaritan or the rich fool—none is found in John's gospel.

Moreover, John alone among the gospel writers arranged Jesus' ministry around a three-year period. There are three distinct Passover celebrations referred to in the book (2:13, 6:4, 11:55). This contrasts sharply with the view of the three earlier synoptic gospels that Jesus' ministry lasted little more than a year.

When we notice all that John omitted in his retelling of the story and all that he rearranged, we wonder why he bothered to write another gospel. Based on what we know from the synoptic gospels, he did not tell the story very well. Is this because the author was John, the disciple, and by the time of this writing he is quite old and forgetful? The gospel itself claims to have been written by "that disciple whom Jesus loved"; that is, John (John 21:20-24), but modern scholars are uncertain. Whoever was the author, we would like to ask him a question or two about his work. "John," we want to say, "why bother to tell the story again if you leave so much of it out? You don't tell us about Jesus' birth or his baptism. You don't give us a single parable. What was your purpose in writing another gospel?"

The gospel, itself, states the author's purpose. It was written, he said, "that you may believe that Jesus is the Christ, the Son of God, and that believing you may have life in his name." (John 20:31) But knowing something of the historical context that gave rise to a fourth gospel, we may elaborate a bit on that briefly stated purpose.

Let us imagine that John were with us today and that he stood up to explain his gospel. He might say something like this: "Listen, I didn't want to write another gospel, but circumstances demanded it. I was well satisfied with the stories written by Mark and Matthew and Luke, and it was not until nearly 100 AD that I felt obliged to write another version of the story.

"Let me tell you why. Two things happened near the end of that first century, things that threatened the life of the Church. First, there arose a heresy in the Church, and many of our people were affected by it. The movement was called 'gnosticism,' and its proponents believed that everything material was evil. The world was evil, body and matter were evil, and only the spiritual was good. They even began to say that Jesus wasn't really human; he only appeared to be, they said. He had no body. He was not flesh and blood, only spirit. Now when they began to preach that Jesus had no physical body and was only spirit, I knew better than that, and so I had to write my gospel.

"The other thing that happened was this. By 100 AD, it had become apparent that the future of the Church would not be found among the Jews. They were rejecting the Gospel. If the Church was going to flourish, it would have to be among the Gentiles, and none of the other gospels appealed particularly to the Greeks. Their tradition had no thought of a Messiah, whatever, and the other gospels emphasized the messianic role of Jesus. So I had to find a way to tell the story of Jesus in such a way that the Gentiles would believe in him. This is what I tried to do in my gospel, and this is why it is so different from the other three."

Hearing this explanation from John, let us check and see how well he did. First, he rejected the idea that the world was evil, that everything material was bad. The best known verse in his gospel, perhaps in the entire New Testament, says this very clearly: "For God so loved the *world* that he gave his only Son. . . ." (John 3:16 [Italics added]) It wasn't just the Church which God loved, but his whole created world. It was not evil.

And Jesus himself was flesh and blood; not wispy spirit, but muscle and sinew and bone. "And the Word became flesh," John said, "and dwelt among us. . . ." (John 1:14) John, more than any other gospel writer, stressed the humanity of Jesus. In his gospel, John pictures Jesus becoming angry (2:15), growing tired (4:6), getting hungry (4:31), showing sorrow and grief (11:33), growing thirsty (19:28). Only in John do we find the note about the soldier, after the Crucifixion, piercing Jesus' side with a spear and shedding blood as a result (19:34). Jesus was clearly flesh and blood, and John wanted to testify to that.

John's second purpose was to present the good news in terms the people in the Greek world, the Gentiles, could understand. They cared little for the idea of a Messiah, so it was useless to assert to them that Jesus was the long-sought anointed one from God. They had never sought a Messiah. But they did have a tremendous interest in knowing what God was like. Plato, in particular, centuries before had speculated about God's nature, and one term in particular was used by the Greek philosophers in describing God. "He was," they said, "the Logos, the Word, the perfect Word which had brought all the world into being."

The Greeks, then, often spoke of God as "the Word." This title came to mean "the mind of God" in Greek philosophy. Through this door, John carried the gospel into Greek thinking. "You Greeks for centuries have talked about the Logos, the Word, the mind of God. I tell you that the Word has become flesh and for a time dwelt among us. The mind of God became a person, and that person was this Jesus of Nazareth. Do you really want to know what God is like? Listen, while I tell you, for that Word made flesh was Jesus of Nazareth."

In some ancient study, then, an old and feeble man named John sat down and dictated what he remembered of Jesus of Nazareth. There was no need to repeat the parables; they were already well told by Luke and

Matthew. There was no need to include every incident of Jesus' life; Mark had done that very well. The great need was to tell a struggling and anxious Gentile world what God was like, and this is what John set out to do. "And the Word became flesh and dwelt among us . . . .," "In him was life, and the life was the light of men." (John 1:14, 4)

Who among us needs that message today? Only those who feel an emptiness inside that things cannot fill. Only those in whom some instinct burns that turns them toward God. Only those for whom human strength runs out. Only the anxious, the guilty, the lonely, the afraid. Only, in short, those who dwell in some kind of personal darkness, for John is the gospel of light. More than twenty times, he uses this figure of speech: light in darkness. This is what God is like, he was saying, the giver of light. Centuries before, the prophet Isaiah had said it: "The people who walked in darkness have seen a great light; those who dwelt in a land of deep darkness, on them has light shined." (Isaiah 9:2)

John takes up that message and puts it in terms comprehensible to the Gentile world. Who among us does not need it today? Who among us does not know periods of darkness when the light seems distant and gone? "There is light for whatever darkness you are now in," John said. "God has sent it." John states it over and again: "In him was life, and the life was the light of men. The light shines in the darkness, and the darkness has not overcome it." (1:4, 5) "The true light that enlightens every man was coming into the world." (1:9) "I am the light of the world," said Jesus, "he who follows me will not walk in darkness, but will have the light of life." (8:12) "While you have the light, believe in the light, that you may become sons of light." (12:36) "I have come as light into the world, that whoever believes in me may not remain in darkness." (12:46)

Do you see why it is called the gospel of light? "Light in darkness," it says! "Light come to all persons!" Is this not our need today? Surely there is not a single area of darkness that any of us experiences that John himself had not lived through. He was probably ninety years old when his gospel was written. Did he, perhaps, know something of the darkness of fading vision? Did he not know that his life was running out? To those of us who share with him the knowledge that much of life is past, the message is clear: however great the darkness, there is the light of God shining clearly in its midst, and the darkness cannot ever put it out.

Some of us bear burdens of guilt, and John knew that, too. He, with all the others, ran away when Jesus was crucified. He was the "beloved" disciple; yet at Jesus' trial, he was in hiding. Is it the darkness of guilt that bothers us? John knew it, and yet after years of remembering his guilt, he could still say that there is light shining even in the darkness of guilt.

Is it the darkness of sin that overcomes us? Are we caught up in some dark habit of life that we cannot break? "He who follows me will not walk in darkness, but will have the light of life," Jesus said (8:12).

Listen, if we haven't heard the Gospel in a long time, this is it! This is the Good News! No matter how great the darkness seems to you, there is light, there is hope, there is mercy and forgiveness and joy, and this is what the Gospel means. If Christian faith means to you guilt and condemnation and grief, then purge it of these meanings. If it means to you punishment and accusation and darkness, then away with it. If it has for you more weight than wings, then listen to John's gospel and rejoice in what he says: "For God so loved the world that he gave his only Son, that whoever believes in him should not perish, but have eternal life." (3:16) "I have come as light into the world, that whoever believes in me may not remain in darkness." (12:46)

What is your darkness right now? Guilt? Anxiety? Doubt? Fear? What is it? The Gospel says that whatever it is, however dark it may be, the light of God can shine right into it and through it, and can bring light to your life. There *is* no darkness so deep that the love of God cannot shine into it and bring light and love and joy to life.

It is said that when the ancient Greeks built their little ships, in a formal ceremony, they erected the mast. Always underneath the mast, the shipbuilders placed a gold coin, so that even when the ship was wrecked there would always be something of value left hidden down there under the mast, deep under the darkness of the sea.

When you and I were created, that gold coin—God's image—was placed within us. No matter how complete the wreckage of our own life may seem there is buried there deep within us that bit of gold, and God won't let it go. He seeks it in his children right now, calling us to walk in the light of life and making us a solemn promise: "The light shines in the darkness, and the darkness has not overcome it." (1:5)

11 ACTS
Is the Church Good for Christianity?

Now what kind of question is that? "Is the Church good for Christianity?" Here I have gone to great effort to get myself up, get the children ready, drive up here to church and find a parking place, come in, and the preacher asks, as though there were any doubt about it, "Is the Church good for Christianity?" It's like hearing the president of Local 38 asking, "Are unions good for Labor?" or hearing the Speaker of the House ask, "Is Congress good for government?" *Of course* the Church is good for Christianity, isn't it? And yet, consider some disturbing facts.

Among some circles of younger people, there's a lot of respect for Jesus, but not much admiration for the Church. Consider the popularity in recent years of such hit musicals as *Godspell* and *Jesus Christ, Superstar* and films like Zeffirelli's *Jesus of Nazareth.* There are Jesus festivals and rallies and movements galore, and at one such rally a student carried a banner that said, "Jesus Yes, Church No!" *Is* the Church good for Christianity? Moreover, some of the fastest growing Christian groups are not only non-church-related; they are in some cases anti-church, encouraging youth participation in the group but not always leading them to participation in local churches. Such non-church-related groups as Young Life, Campus Crusade, Youth for Christ, and Inter-Varsity Fellowship are flourishing. In addition to this, there is the popularity of electronic religion where skilled communicators draw vast followings from people, many of whom give little support to any specific local congregation. Such supporters of the electronic church give almost a quarter of a billion dollars a year to these programs.

Given the fact that so many people give such loyal support to these non-church movements, ask it again, "What kind of job *is* the Church doing for Christianity?" A sober critic like Soren Kierkegaard said it decades ago: "Whereas Jesus turned water into wine, the Church has succeeded in doing something more difficult: it has turned wine into water."

Today, we put the Church under the microscope and give it a careful evaluation. We cannot use direct words of Jesus in this evaluation, because in all four gospels Jesus is quoted as using the word "church" only twice (Matt. 16:18, 18:17). But there is an exciting book in the New Testament that does use the word often, telling us in detail about the birth of the Church. That book is Acts, the Acts of the Apostles, and it brings life both to us as individuals and to our churches. What does it offer us?

Start with a quick look at the background of the book and a summary. The first verse of the book quickly reminds the reader of the first verses of the gospel according to Luke and, thus, identifies the author. Luke was an occasional companion of Paul in his journeys. For the most part, Acts is written in the third person plural. We hear that *they* went to Phrygia. But Acts 16:11 abruptly switches to a first person plural narrative: "*We* made a direct voyage to Samothrace. . . ." Luke apparently joined Paul's party there and eventually went with him to Rome. Acts, then, is a second volume which continues the story Luke began with his gospel.

It is a fast-paced book, one with its share and more of murder and intrigue, heroism and adventure. The book's main purpose is to tell how the Church began. It tells what the disciples did in those first days after the crucifixion, how they set about telling of Jesus and winning followers to his cause. At first, they met in the temple courtyard, but an unfavorable response by the Jewish authorities forced them out (Acts 1-4).

The Christian movement soon spread to other communities, and a dramatic turn came when one of the Church's worst enemies, Saul of Tarsus, himself became a Christian (Acts 9). Most of the book tells about Paul's travels about the Mediterranean world, complete with shipwreck and imprisonment and all that went with such adventures. By the time the book ends, the Church is thirty years old, and a strange phenomenon has become evident. The stronger the Church became, the more hidden became Jesus Christ within it.

How can one explain this phenomenon? It says something about our question, "Is the Church good for Christianity?" There was never a time in its history when the Church was more vigorous and alive than those first difficult years when it was being persecuted on every hand, when it was struggling for some structure and working for followers. But as the Church grew stronger, as it gained a large following and a measure of respectability, as it became well-organized and set up clear rules of conduct and procedure, as it did all this, the Jesus for whom the Church was called into being started receding into the background. This progression culminated a few centuries later when the Holy Catholic Church became absolute ruler of all Europe, with its power matched only by its corruption, and Jesus Christ hidden completely behind its structured power.

What we see in Acts is a process that takes place in every human endeavor: *the tendency of the organization to become more important than the cause for which it was founded,* the tendency of the vessel to become more important than its contents. No matter how Christ-centered it was in the beginning, the Church and its organization soon came to be more important than the Christ it was created to serve.

This is a group dynamic not limited to the Church. A moment ago we tried to imagine a labor leader asking, "Are unions good for Labor?" And yet, the same process has happened here. In 1982, the Labor movement in the United States celebrated its one hundredth anniversary, and union membership has declined from 40% of the working force twenty years ago to 25% today. Critics within the movement claim that the union and its maintenance has become more important than the demands for equity and justice it was formed to champion.

Similarly, we tried to imagine the Speaker of the House asking, "Is Congress good for government?" Yet Jimmy Carter ran successfully for the presidency in 1976, arguing that Congress had forgotten its original reason for being, that it no longer served the people it represented.

Any human endeavor is subject to the same dynamic. A great cause emerges in history. It attracts followers who organize to promote that cause, and as years pass, the organization—its buildings and budgets and offices and programs—becomes more important than the cause which brought it into being.

Occasionally, the same process is seen even in the home. The house, which was intended to shelter a home and provide a setting for a family to grow together, becomes more important than the home within it. I once knew a fine woman who had long wanted white carpets in her living and dining rooms. One day she got them, and their protection became the most important cause in her life. I visited her one day, entered the front door, and saw black runners she had placed over those white carpets from the front door back to the family room. It tested her diplomacy to find a way to tell the visiting minister that he was not to step off the runners onto the carpet, but she did. So far as I know, to this day the white carpets have never been trod on by mortal foot. The house became more important than the home it sheltered, for there was no dining in the dining room and no living in the living room.

The reason, then, that sometimes the Church isn't good for Christianity is that it tends to become more important than the Christ who brought it into being. This happens in so many ways. Almost every community has its problems with the case of the Christmas display that went beserk in someone's yard and began to grow like Jack's beanstalk. At first it seemed harmless enough, a few colored bulbs strung up around a porch, but that was only the beginning. As years passed, the colored lights crept all around the house, up the chimney, and over the roof. A gadget that made the lights blink off and on was attached. A manger scene sprouted on the front lawn, and the herd around the manger grew constantly. As alarmed neighbors watched, Santa Claus appeared at the chimney and then his sled and reindeer, with the reindeer heads nodding and the harness jingling. Little animals of every sort, mechanized to move in rhythm, soon were added, and loudspeakers presented music for it all. Soon it was a cacaphony of sound and motion, with a new ride added every year by the proud owner.

What had started as a modest bit of beauty to light up the cold winter darkness in honor of Jesus' birth was now a gaudy show, and down that residential street came cars from all over the country. Neighbors gritted their teeth as the horns honked and the fast food wrappers flew and the drivers shook their fists at one another—all almost drowned out by the sounds of the Christmas display gone mad, a display whose maintenance became more important than the Christ whose birth it was meant to honor.

In a less exaggerated way, this happens to the Church, and the more it happens, the more hidden the Christ within becomes. Are there symptoms of this we need to watch for? Consider these.

First, *the Church today is bad for Christianity when it becomes so locked in to its old ways that it refuses change.* It is good for Christianity when it not only permits, but reaches for, constructive change. After all, had those earliest Christians not been willing to change radically their own religious faith, there never would have been a Church. I sometimes wonder, in a bit of fantasizing, what would happen if all of us were somehow picked up and set down in Jerusalem in 33 AD. Would *we* have been open enough to change to become followers of Christ? It was a radical step for them to take—actually to claim that this Jesus of Nazareth was the Son of God.

Their faith demanded other changes. They had to move from worship in the temple to worship in homes, to welcome Gentiles into the circle of believers, to abandon some old Jewish customs long held important. The Church flourished as long as they were willing to change. But as the organization became more important than its message, change became more difficult. There have always been those who see the Church as a club with a clubhouse, not to be disturbed. And when change comes, as inevitably it must, there are always those who make lonely journeys in their later years, moving from one church to another in a poignant search for yesterday's world.

We today face so many changes in our society that we must be open to creative changes in how we operate. Some of the changes we face are the huge increase in the number of women who work outside the home, the increase in leisure time, the rapid development of the electronic church, the ravage of inflation, the stresses of the energy crisis, the development of computers and electronic learning aids, and so many more. Does the Church pretend that nothing ever changes in the setting of its world, or does it devise new forms and methods for presenting the Gospel of Christ? To the degree that the Church is willing to change as needed, it is good for Christianity.

A second symptom: the Church is bad for Christianity when it is unwilling aggressively to search for and then to assimilate new members in its midst. It is good for Christianity when its doors are open, with new people being constantly drawn in. Yet, one of the first crises the disciples faced involved this very issue. They had arranged things rather neatly for themselves in Jerusalem. There was a respectable number of members there. The organization was set and the disciples were in control. Then, suddenly, here came a new person with new ideas. It was Paul—not one of them, yet claiming that he believed, too—wanting to work for Christ in the church. They accepted him very reluctantly, and as soon as they could they sent him way up north to do all the preaching he wanted to do. "Way up north" turned out to be Asia Minor and Europe, the Gentile world, and soon Paul had more converts in a dozen churches than there were in all of Jerusalem put together. And that's where the future of the Church was to be found. To the degree that it reaches out for new people, the Church is good for Christianity.

One last symptom: the Church is good for Christianity when it is seen as something to be used to enrich life. We are not to use our lives for the purpose of making the Church strong; we are to use the Church for the purpose of making our lives strong. The Church is a factory, a machine, a tool, intended to be taken and used to meet the needs of our lives.

In communities across the nation every autumn, we spend the weekends watching our teams play football. As vigorous as that sport is, our going and watching really doesn't add to our physical health. A football game is usually twenty-two persons needing rest performing in front of sixty thousand people needing exercise. We go to the game to watch good athletes in the fine condition which we will never achieve.

Is that the Church's purpose? Do we come here to watch people being religious? No! The Church is not to be watched, or honored, or revered so much as it is to be used. The Church is good for Christianity if you, through it, find Jesus Christ touching your life in the area of your specific need. Does it lift you up when you are low and direct you when you are without purpose? Does it give you a presence when you are lonely and hope when you are discouraged? Does it make you examine your old prejudices in the light of Christ's love? Does it open your eyes to the hurts of those who suffer injustice? Does it make you grow?

Once in Colorado on vacation, I found a detective book on a shelf and immediately was caught up in it and captured by its exciting story. Several hours of reading later, I discovered that the final three or four pages, which included the solution to the mystery, were gone. Someone had ripped them out long ago. I never found out the solution to that interrupted story.

The book of Acts concludes that way: no ending at all! Was Paul ever released from prison in Rome? Was he executed there? What finally happened to the Church? We don't know. The book concludes not with "The End," but with "To Be Continued." And it is continued, that story, in your life and mine. By what we do with this Church put into our hands, we give our own answer to the question, "Is the Church good for Christianity?"

12 THESSALONIANS
Present-Tense Religion

The Christian Church in the Greek city of Thessalonica was in trouble, and something had to be done about it. No, they were not trying to get rid of their minister. They were not arguing over a building program, or the National Council of Churches, or what curriculum to use in their Sunday school. Their problem was, in a sense, a theological one, and the whole church was stirred up about it.

The church was only a couple of years old. It had been established by Paul about the year 50 AD, but Paul had left and gone on to other cities, and the church at Thessalonica was left to shift for itself. With only the memories of what Paul had taught them, the Thessalonian people had strayed down a side road of the Gospel and had centered all their religious thinking on the second coming of Jesus. And that is a difficult subject, at best. Down in Central Texas, where the fog is particularly bad, an old rancher told of shingling his barn in a fog so thick that before he knew what he was doing he had shingled four rows of fog onto his barn. There is probably no subject in Christian thinking in which it is easier to go shingling off into the fog than this one, the second coming of Christ.

The people in Thessalonica remembered that Paul had taught that someday Christ would come again, and they were impatiently waiting on that Second Coming. They had been preaching to all the pagan people in the town that the Lord was on his way and that quite soon they would be taken straight to heaven, leaving all the cares of the world behind them.

But months had passed and nothing had happened. The townspeople were beginning to poke fun at them. "Where's this Jesus you've been looking for?" they were asking. "He's running late, isn't he?" In addition to this, the Thessalonian Christians were worried about some of their own people who had died since Paul had established the Church. They were dead and buried, and it looked like they would miss the great coming of the Lord. What was going to happen to them?

Some of the Thessalonians were taking so seriously the belief that Jesus might return at any moment that they had quit their jobs and were spending full-time sitting and waiting. They didn't work at all and depended on the other folks in the church to feed them. This was causing not just a little bit of trouble in the church, and this was the situation when Timothy, Paul's young associate minister, came walking into Thessalonica one day.

Paul had sent Timothy back to find out what was going on at Thessalonica, and Timothy found out quickly. After checking with the folk there, he realized immediately that things weren't going well with the church, and he returned quickly to Paul to give him a report. "They're future-tense people," Timothy might have said to Paul. "All they talk about is the Second Coming, when and how and where it's going to be. All their faith centers in on what's going to happen someday."

So Paul sat down and wrote them a letter—two letters, in fact. And in his letters, he attempted to pull them back to the present moment and recognize that Christianity was first of all a present-tense religion. "Listen," he wrote them, "don't worry about those who have already died; they will be taken care of when the Lord comes again, just as those who are still left will be." But Paul said it was a waste of time to speculate about all this. "About dates and times," he wrote, "you have no need to have anything written to you, for you know all you need to know, that the Lord will come unexpectedly." (I Thess. 5:1-2)

In his second letter, Paul repeated the instruction. "Now brothers," he wrote, "about the coming of our Lord Jesus Christ and his gathering of us to himself: I beg you, don't lose your heads or alarm yourselves." (II Thess. 2:1-2) And get one thing straight, he said, "The man who will not work shall not eat." (II Thess. 3:10)

Having spoken about the relative importance of this subject, Paul reminds them of their obligations to live obediently in *this* day and *this* age. He discussed personal integrity and responsibility. He mentioned idleness and gossip and lust and pride and selfishness. He called the Thessalonian people back to the present tense and said, "Behold, now is the acceptable time; behold, now is the day of salvation." (II Cor. 6:2)

Here, then, 2,000 years later is Paul's letter to a struggling church, and what does it have to do with us? Are these letters simply museum pieces, to be looked at from afar, reflections of a quaint faith in a quaint age? Not quite! It is remarkable how aptly the letters fit the religious situation among us today. Not too many years ago, Hal Lindsay wrote a book which made a lot of money. The book was called *The Late, Great Planet Earth,* and it rode the crest of a religious phenomenon which occurs in cycles among Christians, appearing every time the international situation becomes tense and people become anxious over the state of things about them. Is the world about to end? Is the second coming of Christ at hand? Does prophecy identify our generation as the last one?

Many Christians, dwelling in a land where human need is evident and opportunities for service great, chose to center their thinking on a completely non-biblical word called "Rapture"—a time when they would suddenly be lifted up and taken away from all the aching needs of the world. Lindsey's book attempted to prove in detail the answer people were wanting to hear: Yes, the end of time is at hand. Any moment, now, the trumpets would sound, and the evil Russians and Chinese would all die horrible deaths, and it would be all halos and soft clouds for the followers of Jesus Christ. God's chosen people would be raised straight to glory.

Lindsey's book simply milked the profits from this wider movement among Christian people. It offered an escape religion, trading on our unwillingness to accept responsibility for living compassionate lives here and now. The end result is that a host of Christian people today find themselves living in the future tense just as the Thessalonians were doing when Paul wrote to them.

Now really, what difference does it make? If some folk want to center their religious lives around neat little systems about the end of the world and their dream of future glory, what difference does it make? Very little, perhaps, unless you find yourself in the grip of someone who confidently and dogmatically offers you a timetable for eternity and implies that unless you accept that sort of thinking you are less than Christian. If that happens to you, here are some things to remember.

First, such speculation about when and where and how God will close down the shop on this earth is non-biblical, even anti-biblical. In Mark 13:31, 32, Jesus says to his friends, "Heaven and earth will pass away. . . . But of that day or that hour *no one knows, not even the angels in heaven, nor the Son, but only the Father.*" [Italics added] He repeats this in Matt. 24:36: "But of that day and hour no one knows, not even the angels of heaven, nor the Son, but the Father only."

Or, look to Acts 1:7, where Jesus responds to a question the disciples put to him: "It is not for you to know times or seasons which the Father has fixed by his own authority." Isn't it strange? Despite the fact that Jesus said the angels don't know when, and even *he* didn't know when, and that it isn't for *us* to know when, there are so many persons running around today, saying, "*I* know when." The clear biblical teaching is this—that when you start speculating about signs of the end, when and where and how, you are "coloring far outside the lines" and entering into a matter Jesus says belongs only to God.

Consider another reason for avoiding such speculation. Paul stressed it to the Thessalonians. The more attention they gave to the speculations about the future, the worse job they were doing living in the present. Isn't it remarkable that after Paul said a word to the Thessalonians about their fascination with the second coming of Christ, he had to add a word like this: (Listen to it!) "This is the will of God, that you must be holy; you must abstain from fornication; each one of you must learn to gain mastery over his body, to hallow and honor it, not giving way to lust like the pagans who are ignorant of God. . ." (I Thess. 4:3ff.)

No wonder the Thessalonians had rather talk about the Second Coming! Paul, you see, got very personal with them. He spoke to them about life as it was being lived right then and there. He spoke to them about ministering to the needy among them. "Listen," he said, "I want you to support the weak, to encourage the fainthearted. You must live at peace among yourselves." There is always the temptation coming to us in any age to pull Christianity's teeth, to make it irrelevant, to locate it out yonder somewhere in the distant future, to let it concern visions in the sky somewhere, but not the poor and hungry and hopeless and distressed among us.

I have a Korean friend named Peter Suk who often speaks of his life as a Christian in Korea. One night he was telling a group of us why Christianity was able to gain a hearing in Korea. The Buddhist and Confucian religions, he said, tended to stay up on the mountain tops, to deal in mysticism and speculation about the various levels of heaven. But Christianity came into Korea preaching a gospel of human involvement, compassion, and love. It dealt with feeding the starving, sheltering the homeless, teaching the illiterate. And so, throughout Korea, Christianity makes headway.

This is essentially what Paul told the Thessalonians. He was warning them against a toothless, future-centered faith. He was calling them back to a present-tense religion.

And one last reason for centering religious faith in the here and now: If we move through life with eyes fixed on the distant scenery of eternity, we miss the joy of *this* life. The Thessalonians, majoring in what God offers out yonder somewhere, were missing the joy God offers in life right here and now.

No one believed in eternal life more than Paul did, but he was willing to leave that in God's hands. As for now, his mission was to teach obedience and love and faith: it was to serve, to teach, to preach. His calling was to rejoice in what life was offering him then and there. Consequently, when you read his letters, again and again you find these phrases: "I rejoice always. . . .I thank my God. . . .Yes, I shall rejoice. . . .I am glad and I rejoice with you all." You see, if a person truly believes that God stands there in the shadows at the end, ready to receive us to himself, then that person can turn loose of that and live the life of joy here and now.

This ancient book is timely to all of us, because even today we hear echoes of the old Thessalonian problem. We hear those who withdraw from the God-given jobs of this present world and center their faith in sterile speculations about eternity, speculations which do not feed the hungry or clothe the naked or give light to those who walk in darkness. But this modern fascination with the future repeats the ancient error. It goes against the clear teachings of Jesus. It lessens our involvement in the real problems Christians should be dealing with today. And it makes us miss the joy that comes with an involved life of faith today.

An old New England farmer once cleared his land of the rocks that covered it. With those rocks he built a rock fence that was three feet high and four feet wide. When someone asked him why the unusual dimension, three feet high and four feet wide, he said that he built it that way so that if the wind blew the fence over it would be taller than ever before.

That's our call from Christ. Build your life strongly, firmly. Do the best job you can of living concerned and loving lives of obedience here and now. Then, when the winds of eternity blow it over, it will be taller than ever before. For, as Jesus said, "But seek first his kingdom and his righteousness, and all these things shall be yours as well." (Matt. 6:33)

13 PHILIPPIANS
What We All Need Most

Let me introduce you to four people and ask you, "What do these people need most?" First is Mary Ann, a high school junior. For the past two years, Mary Ann has enjoyed going out regularly with Bill. Football games, dances, movies—it was always Bill and Mary Ann. But last week, Bill told her that he was checking out and that he wouldn't be calling her anymore. Now Mary Ann sits home on Friday night and jumps only briefly when the phone rings, because she knows it is not for her.

Next is John, a boy in the tenth grade. Ever since grade school, he has participated in Boys Club basketball. Hour after hour he spent practicing hook shots and jump shots and all the rest. He dreamed about the high school team and college beyond, maybe all-district, maybe even all-state. But yesterday, the high school coach very regretfully cut him from the team. He just didn't have it, and now John is on his way to study hall while the other fellows head for basketball practice.

Third is Bill Smith, who is forty years old. Bill has been with his firm for fourteen years, has done his work well, and has been loyal, conscientious, and dependable. Last week the boss finally announced who was going to be the new vice-president. The promotion went to a thirty-five-year-old fellow who had been with them only four years. Bill is now on his way to the office on Monday morning where the new vice-president will lead the staff meeting for the first time.

Last in line is Mrs. Jones, now 85. She has worked hard in her lifetime. She raised a family of four children, was widowed, and now her health is worsening. It appears that she will have to move into a nursing home. None of the children has room for her; they hardly have time to visit because of such busy schedules they follow. Inflation has eaten away her pension. Now she sits waiting for the man from the nursing home to come by and give her the details about their services, and she sits considering where life has brought her now.

Here are four people, and our question is, "What do they need most?" Easy! Mary needs a boyfriend, John needs a hook shot, Bill a promotion, and Mrs. Jones a place to live. And on the surface, this may be true. But down deep, each one needs what all of us need, the ability to get through life and its disappointments without bitterness, to face life's worst and still have joy and faith.

Read Paul's letter to the Philippians and between every line we see peering at us a man who managed to do just that. It is a letter which radiates serenity and faith and joy. And we know that there was every reason for Paul to have reached this point of his life with bitterness and distress. He had gone through a great deal of personal misery.

Remember the story of the pulpit committee chairman who read this letter to his committee? "Gentlemen," the letter began, "I understand that your pulpit is vacant, and I should like to apply. I am generally considered to be a capable preacher, having been a leader in most of the places I have served. I have found time to do some writing on the side.

"I am over fifty years of age, and although my health is not very good, I still manage to get enough work done to please my people. As for a reference, I am somewhat handicapped. I have never preached in any place for more than two and a half years, and the churches have been small. You might as well know that I had to leave some of the churches because my preaching caused trouble in the town. Where I stayed, I did not get along too well with other religious leaders in the town. I have also been threatened several times and have been physically attacked. Three or four times I have ended up in jail because of my convictions. Still, I feel that I can bring vitality to your church, and I would like to apply for the position."

The committee members were aghast that anyone would think that *their* church could use a middle-aged, trouble-making ex-jailbird. "Who wrote that letter?" they asked. "Well," said the chairman of the committee, "the letter is signed, 'The Apostle Paul'."

And it is all true. When Paul first visited the Greek city of Philippi about 52 AD, he was thrown in jail for the first time in his life. But he organized a church there and then moved on to other cities. In the next ten years, he visited Philippi several times and was generously supported by the Philippian people. Philippi was apparently Paul's favorite church and these were his favorite people. (Acts 16)

But now it is twelve years later, about 64 AD, and Paul has been thrown in prison again, this time in Rome. He is getting old. His health is not good. He faces probable death in prison. He wants desperately to be released so as to realize his one last ambition—to preach the gospel in Spain. So much to do! So little time! But month after month passes and he remains in jail. So one day Paul writes a letter to his friends in

Philippi, and it is this letter that we have today. It is very short, only four chapters long, but it is a jewel of faith.

Knowing something of his situation, we are astounded at the spirit of his letter. Not one trace of bitterness! It's a spirit of joyousness and triumph that we find there. The word "joy" and its equivalents are found more in this one short letter than in all the other letters of Paul put together. In prison, mind you, but joyful! Facing possible execution, but serene! Unable to carry out his ministry, but triumphant! Mary, Bill, John, and Mrs. Jones (and all of us who wilt before far less serious disappointments than these) need to know how he did it. Paul must have had a secret that we haven't fathomed yet.

There's no secret some of us might say. *Look how successful Paul was, how respected.* No wonder he escaped bitterness! But test that out. Successful? Highly respected? That would, indeed, help a person get through a difficult time, but it must not have been Paul's secret. We read of him preaching in Athens, the Greek capital, where he so wanted to make a good impression. Acts tells what happened: "And some of the Epicurean and Stoic philosophers joined issue with him. Some said, 'What can this charlatan be trying to say?' . . . When they heard [him preach], they scoffed!" (Acts 17:18, 32 NEB)

Paul discovered soon enough that he could never please everyone. He discovered that even in those fabled churches of the New Testament there was always someone who didn't like something. And surely, most of our churches continue that New Testament tradition today. Paul would recognize us immediately. Some don't like the new curriculum. Some don't like the anthems the choir sings. Some don't like the preacher to wear a robe. Some don't like the preacher to play golf. And some don't like the preacher, period!

And some didn't like Paul! Paul's secret could not have been that everyone liked him, for they didn't. Someone at Corinth criticized Paul by saying, "His letters. . .are weighty and powerful; but [his bodily presence is weak], and as a speaker he is beneath contempt." (II Cor. 10:10 NEB) "I may be no speaker," Paul says in his own defense, "but knowledge I have." (II Cor. 11:5 NEB) Obviously, it was not universal admiration and unqualified success that prevented bitterness in Paul.

If not that, then *maybe it was his staunch circle of close friends who stood by him to the very end.* Anyone can endure disappointment with this kind of support. Ah, but read his letters and hear the little personal references that are included. Demas was one of his best friends; but, wrote Paul, ". . .Demas, in love with this present world, has deserted me. . . ." (II Tim. 4:9) Barnabas was his partner on his first missionary journey, but Paul had to say to the Galatians, ". . .even Barnabas was carried away and played false like the rest." (Gal. 2:13 NEB) "Everyone in the province of Asia deserted me," he said. (II Tim. 1:15 NEB) "At the first hearing of my case," he wrote again, "no one came into court to support me; they all left me in the lurch. . . ." (II Tim. 4:16 NEB)

If Paul was able to avoid bitterness, it wasn't because all his friends stood by him. He knew disappointment there, too.

What about good health? Most people can make it through life courageously if they are given good health and if they feel good. Perhaps that was Paul's secret.

But no! He wrote to the Corinthians, "To keep me from being unduly elated. . .I was given a sharp physical pain which came as Satan's messenger to bruise me. . . ." (II Cor. 12:7 NEB) "Even when we reached Macedonia," he wrote, "there was still no relief for this poor body. . . ." (II Cor. 7:5 NEB)

Paul knew his share and more of physical suffering. He spoke so often of his "thorn in the flesh" that we know perfect health was not his secret for staying joyful in the face of adversity.

Then if it was not unusual success, if it was not loyal friends, perfect health, or rugged righteousness that led Paul through life unscathed in spirit, what was it? Try this on for answer: It was Paul's deeply felt belief that life was always moving toward a completion, a fulfillment that God would bring, and that all the little disappointments of today are but detours leading to that fulfillment.

The little girl complained to her brother about the mountain trail they were climbing. "There are too many bumps here," she said. "Yes," the brother answered, "but the bumps are what you climb on." So Paul wrote the Philippians from his prison cell: "I want you to know, brethren, that what has happened to me has really served to advance the gospel. . . .and most of the brethren have been made confident in the Lord because of my imprisonment. . . ." (Phil 1:12, 14) The bumps are what he climbed on!

This is precisely the theology of one of this century's greatest religious thinkers, the late Teilhard de Chardin. A French anthropologist and theologian, Teilhard saw God's hand and design in all of creation. He was a thoroughgoing evolutionist and saw in the "gropings" of evolution God's divine plan being worked out. All of life is moving through a series of failures and achievements. "Even the blind alleys become meaningful," Teilhard said.[1] The bumps of creation are what we climb on.

Paul used the bumps of life as a scaffold to climb right on up every time he fell. Some forgotten poet once said, "I know I'm wounded, but not slain. I'll lay me down and rest awhile, and then rise up and fight again." It was this attitude that brought Paul through life, and it was this faith he shared with the Philippians. It is what we *all* need most. No failure ever need be final, no disappointment complete. We climb on them. We forget what lies behind. We strain forward to what lies ahead. We press on. No failure is final!

Here is an experience of an eighteen-year-old college freshman. He was considering the ministry, so he joined the college youth group at the church next to the university he was attending. He shared the usual freshman jitters at being a newcomer at a large university, but all the freshmen shared this. The church group met each Sunday night and ended with worship in the sanctuary. It was the custom for a freshman to lead the worship service each time, and early that first year his turn came.

He wanted desperately to do a good job. After all, he was a ministerial student, and he wanted to impress the upper classmen there with his ability. That night after their program, they filed into the darkened sanctuary for worship. They took their seats, the organ music stopped, and it was perfectly quiet. He got up. Sixty pairs of eyes were on him. Suddenly, his well-prepared service went down the drain. It was a disaster. He choked up and simply couldn't get the words out.

Somehow it struggled to an end, and he slipped quickly out before the others, darted into the darkness beside the church, and stood while they all left. He stayed there for awhile making sure they were all gone. Only then did he make his way back to the dormitory room. To his dismay, it was filled with fellows from the youth group. "Where have you been?" they asked. "We've been waiting for you. We're going over for coffee." There was no choice. He went with them. They talked of the football game coming up, of the new dorm being built, of some of their difficult class assignments. No one mentioned the disaster at the church. But when one of them complained about a confusing assignment from one of their teachers, he knew enough about it to clear it up.

When he finished his explanation, one of them said to me, "Brice, if you're so smart, how could you ruin a worship service so completely?" And they all laughed, and I did, too. Through that supportive circle of friends, it became clear again that the bumps are what you climb on! And this, I think, is what Paul was telling his friends at Philippi. "I know how to be abased, and I know how to abound; in any and all circumstances I have learned the secret of facing plenty and hunger, abundance and want." (Phil. 4:12) And how much we need that kind of faith!

There are some right now who have encountered rough going in life. There are some who are facing trouble in marriage, tension with children, problems with parents. There are some who have quite unexpectedly encountered frustration in life and doubt and despair. There are some in hospital beds, and it's not a bump they have been given but a whole mountain to climb. And there are those who are climbing it! They have found what we all need most, the ability to take the worst that life can throw at us and throw it right back.

From two thousand years back, it's a letter to all of us who face disappointment, and it says: "Life is bumpy, to be sure, but climb on those bumps. Don't give up!" But let Paul himself say it best: "Brethren, I do not consider that I have made it my own; but one thing I do, forgetting what lies behind and straining forward to what lies ahead, I press on toward the goal for the prize of the upward call of God in Christ Jesus." (Phil. 3:13-14)

In the final sense, that kind of faith is what we all need most.

14 COLOSSIANS
Wholehearted Church, Wholehearted People

The minister of the church in Colossae, a small town in Asia Minor, had arrived in Rome, and there was one thing he wanted to do most of all. Visiting the Coliseum and the Forum may have been high on his list, but most important of all was a visit with Paul of Tarsus, the great Christian apostle whose fame had spread throughout the churches of the Roman Empire. This great Christian missionary was in Rome, and Epaphras, the visiting minister, wanted to see him.

So one day in this year of 61 AD, Epaphras put on his best robe, shined his sandals, and went to the place where leading Christians were found most often in those days: the Roman jail. Paul was a prisoner of the Roman government and had been for the several months since his arrival from Jerusalem. Prison arrangements were quite informal, then, especially for Roman citizens such as Paul, and leisurely visits could be made. Probably Paul had been able to rent a private room for himself at the prison, and into that room came the preacher from the small town of Colossae. Epaphras introduced himself to the legendary missionary Paul.

What do you suppose they talked about? I think I know! They likely talked about what preachers still talk about when they get together: their churches. How is your church doing? What is going on there? That, I suspect, is the question Paul put to Epaphras as the conversation began. "Epaphras, how are things going with the church at Colossae?"

And the answer, no doubt, came back: "Tremendous! Terrific! You ought to see the faith of those people. They can't be beat." Such is the nature of casual ministerial conversation. But as the conversation went further, Paul may have voiced the question a second time, "How is your church doing?" And Epaphras may have answered, "Fine, good. They are a fine group of people to work with."

After more conversation, Paul may have found another way to put the same question: "Epaphras, how *is* the church at Colossae going?" And Epaphras may have answered, "Well, things are all right. Of course, we have problems, just like everyone else." This is the usual pattern of clergy give and take. When the question is asked, "How is the church doing?" the required first answer is, "Great! Tremendous!" It is only after the conversation has gone on for a time and a level of trust has been established that the preacher can begin to admit that there *are* problems, that the church is six months behind in its building payments and the board chairman has just run off with the organist.

Thus, if Paul had asked his question once again, Epaphras may well have sighed deeply and answered, "Paul, we're in desperate trouble. I don't know what to do! Can you help me?"

It is fortunate that such a conversation would have had time to run its course, for truth would have been found in both ends of Epaphras' answer. He did have a fine church with which to work. There were signs of a vital, strong faith in that church at Colossae. But there were problems, too, and the chief of them was that a certain group had come into the church teaching a strange type of Christian faith which was threatening to destroy the unity of the church.

There are references to this heresy in the letter Paul wrote the Colossian church. It seems to have been a type of spiritualism whose proponents suggested that it was necessary to talk with angelic beings and to seek visions in order to know God's will fully. Leaders of this movement apparently taught that certain foods could not be eaten and that certain religious holidays had to be observed (Col. 2:8-10, 16-19). All of this was tearing the church apart, and Epaphras shared his concern with Paul.

He must have said something like this: "Paul, I know that you were not the one who established the church at Colossae. I know, too, that you have never even been in Colossae, but you have heard what I have said about my church. They know of your reputation there, and they would listen to you. Would you consider writing a letter to the folks back home, trying to help them get back on the right path again?"

So Paul sat down and wrote a letter to a church he had never visited before, a church in trouble. What advice did he give them?

He might have told them to get a new preacher. "Listen," he might have written, "somehow you got Brother Epaphras over here to Rome. Whatever you do, don't send him a return ticket! I have talked with him and I know! He's a loser, and your church isn't ever going to do any good with him around. If you want to solve your problems, get rid of Brother Epaphras." Churches *have* been known to do this. The minister goes on vacation and gets a letter from the church, saying, "Dear Former Minister, where do you want your furniture sent?" Paul did not advise this. Indeed, he commended Epaphras as being a faithful minister of Christ (Col. 1:7).

Nor did he suggest that they start a building program at Colossae. This often gets the attention and enthusiasm of the people and keeps them excited enough that they have little time left for religion of any sort, heretical or orthodox. But the churches of this period had no buildings of their own. They met in the homes of their members. No building was necessary, so Paul gave no such advice.

He might have urged that they reorganize themselves, write a new constitution, get new committee chairmen or new committees. Not Paul. Instead, he sat down and began to write, "From Paul, apostle of Christ Jesus commissioned by the will of God, . . .to God's people at Colossae, brothers in the faith, incorporate in Christ. Grace to you and peace from God our Father." (Col. 1:1-2 NEB)

The salutation over, Paul begins. Loosely translated, here is what he wrote: "Epaphras has told me what fine people you are in Colossae. Your faith and the fruit of your labor is well known. But he has also told me that there are those among you who are forgetting your basic faith in Christ and that the whole church is losing some of its zeal because of this. Although I have never been in Colossae and most of you have never even seen my face, I am with you in spirit, and I want to give you some advice."

Then follows the body of the letter—the second and third chapters—containing some very pointed words. "Therefore, since Jesus was delivered to you as Christ and Lord, live your lives in union with him." (Col. 2:6 NEB) This is a message Paul has repeated elsewhere, and it was needed at Colossae. To the people at Galatia, he had said, ". . .the only thing that counts is new creation!" (Gal. 6:15 NEB) To the people at Corinth he had written, ". . .if anyone is in Christ, he is a new creation; the old has passed away, behold, the new has come." (II Cor. 5:17)

If you want to know what is wrong with your church, Paul was saying, look to yourselves! You cannot have a wholehearted church made up of halfhearted people. The true church of Jesus Christ is made up of persons who are "new creatures" being constantly renewed in the image of their creator. When Paul discusses the health of the church, he looks first to the commitment and zeal of its members. "You are going to be vulnerable to dissension and heresy and apathy when you forget what faith requires. You received Christ Jesus the Lord—now live in him!"

Then let us face these facts for our own generation. Whenever we feel that the church is not doing what it should do, is not being what it should be, Paul's word to the Colossians applies to us. Yet, it is not an answer that we like to hear. We would prefer that he say, "Listen, these are bad times, indeed, and your church is inevitably reflecting the uncertainty of its culture." Or, we would prefer that he say, "Listen, we have a brand new form of church structure coming out of Jerusalem. Manuals will be mailed shortly, and your problems will be solved." We would prefer that he say almost anything except, "Look to your own faith!"

A psychologist tells of conducting group discussions with a number of couples who were experiencing marital problems. He put the wives in one room and asked them to discuss the shortcomings of their husbands. They responded with eagerness, and he had to end the session long before they were ready. He put the husbands in another room and asked them to list the failings of their wives. They responded enthusiastically, observing how great psychology was and how skilled was the counselor. He then asked each group to discuss, in detail, *their own* shortcomings. The result, in both rooms, was almost total silence. In any setting, we prefer to find the blame elsewhere than in ourselves.

As we analyze the shortcomings of the Church today, we would like for Paul to help us find the blame *out there* somewhere, but he does not do that. Instead, he says, "It is new-creation people who make up the authentic church. You will never have a good church made up of bad people. The authentic church is made up of new-creation people." And in all honesty, do most of us want an authentic church that much? We are willing to remodel our lives slightly, to make some adjustments in our way of living, to move the furniture around a bit, but new creations? Not quite!

Evidence of this is seen in the present-day vulnerability of Christian people to wander after strange varieties of religious experience, just as the Colossians were doing. We have remodeled our lives slightly in order to fit in Christianity but our faith seems empty and without life. So we give ourselves to the exotic outgrowths of faith, primitive gifts of the spirit, and teenage gurus who come with utterly absurd teachings, and amazingly self-righteous groups of twentieth century Pharisees who set themselves up as God. We are vulnerable to all these because they offer us a substitute for the ultimate demand of the Gospel, that we become new creatures. They help us to remodel our lives, adding another religious appliance here and there—rather than becoming new creatures by giving our lives fully to Christ Jesus.

Listen, said Paul, you received Christ—now live in him! There is no substitute for that. You do not need angels and visions and strange spiritual visitations. You need to be new creatures, giving yourself afresh to Christ and letting him live in your daily life. "Let the message of Christ dwell among you in all its richness. Instruct and admonish each other with the utmost wisdom. Sing thankfully in your hearts to God, with psalms and hymns and spiritual songs." (Col. 3:16 NEB)

Paul's word to the Colossians is God's word to the Church today, and to its people. It concerns the "new nature, which is being constantly renewed in the image of its Creator. . . ." (Col. 3:10 NEB) It concerns newness of life. The reason we still have tensions in our churches and problems at home and within ourselves is that we are old creatures walking around with the new name of Christ. We are BC people living in an AD world. We are not new creatures, walking with joy and excitement in the newness of life, but persons of the old nature, walking about with the new name. We are not secure in the arms of God's love. We do not forgive. We do not tolerate. We do not seek peace. We are not compassionate. We do not rejoice in our faith. We are so often bitter and malicious and easy to offend and quick to condemn and criticize, and all this because so many of us are not new creatures at all.

Surely Paul's message to the Colossians reaches across these centuries to us today, saying that many of us who have been in the Church for years still have need of being converted to the new life of love in Jesus Christ. We need to open our hearts to him and let him come in and make new creatures of us.

Those of us who have been in assorted churches for many years, isn't it time we opened our hearts to Christ and began to live like his people—to work and give and pray like his people? This is what Christ's Church needs today—new creatures, walking in newness of life. So enough of patches! Enough of minor remodeling jobs on character! Enough of talking about new techniques, when it is new people we need. Enough of talking about new curriculum or new methods of working with youth, or clever ways for husbands and wives to relate. We don't need new methods and new techniques as much as we need families who will walk in newness of life.

Paul's message to the Colossian church is that there is no shortcut to church renewal and no easy answer to hard problems of church life. The only way to strengthen a church is to strengthen the commitment of its people to Jesus Christ. A wholehearted church requires wholehearted people. "Therefore, since Jesus was delivered to you as Christ and Lord, live your lives in union with him. Be rooted in him; be built in him; be consolidated in the faith you were taught; let your hearts overflow with thankfulness." (Col. 2:6-7 NEB)

Do we want a wholehearted church that much?

15 PETER
Refuge in a Stormy Sea

Suppose you stop one day for a cup of coffee somewhere and an acquaintance joins you; before you know it he is sharing his problems with you. "Bill," he says, "I've about come to the end of my rope, and I don't know whether I can go on or not. My boss says that unless my sales increase he will have to let me go. My wife is on the point of leaving me, and the children are having problems. Bill," he says, "I'm desperate!"

Now you came in for a cup of coffee, and nothing more, but suddenly you are a counselor. In your hands is someone desperate and in trouble. What do you say? Some of the things we say in such situations as this are less than helpful.

"Joe," you say, "you think *you've* got problems? You think that's a bad story? You ought to hear about some of the things I've been going through." And with that, you excuse yourself and leave.

Or, "Come on, cheer up, Joe. That isn't so bad. Everything's going to be just fine, no problem. It will work out all right. Things usually do." And as quickly as you can, you grab your check and leave.

Or, "Yes, Joe, I know just how you feel." A woman in labor was once surprised when the male obstetrician patted her on the shoulder and said soothingly, "There, there, I know just how you feel." This is what you are saying to Joe as you rise to leave.

In short, someone in real desperation has come to you for encouragement, and how have you responded? The way we respond may be helpful, or it may not.

The two letters written by Peter in the New Testament are in response to a desperate situation that existed among the small Christian churches with which he was acquainted in the area of Asia Minor—what we today call Turkey. The people there were in trouble. The boss, which was the Roman Empire, was threatening to fire them, quite literally. The children, in this case the members of the churches, were threatening to run away. In some way, the leaders of the churches of Asia Minor shared their concern with Simon Peter and voiced their fear and anxiety. "What can we do?" they were asking.

Peter was living in Rome, and when he heard of the desperation of the little churches in Asia Minor he wrote these letters of hope and encouragement. His purpose was to bolster the faith of these terrified Christians. What was their problem? They were living under the constant threat of imprisonment or execution by the Roman authorities. Peter referred to their situation several times in his letter. "The end of all things is at hand; . . . ." he said. (I Pet. 4:7) "Beloved, do not be surprised at the fiery ordeal which comes upon you. . . ." (I Pet. 4:12) ". . .now for a little while you may have to suffer various trials,. . . ." (I Pet. 1:6)

Peter knew how afraid they were, and he wrote these two letters to strengthen them. How does he do it? What is *his* strategy as he tries to bolster the faith of those anxious Christians?

One of his strategies was the attempt to explain to those Christian people why they were suffering. There is something instinctive in us that makes us want to know why undeserved suffering comes. Why is this happening? Many persons recently have become acquainted with a book written by Harold Kushner on this subject. The book is entitled *When Bad Things Happen to Good People.* Having experienced a personal family tragedy himself, Rabbi Kushner discusses in detail the different approaches religious people have taken to this problem and arrives at answers that bring at least some satisfaction. Why *do* bad things happen to good people? Why *is* the church in Asia Minor suffering? Peter's first strategy was to offer several explanations. "You are suffering," he said, "so that your faith may be tested and refined. This testing is a reminder to you to live good lives and not give the Gentiles an occasion for persecuting you. When you suffer for righteousness, you are doing just what Christ did. Besides, this means that God's judgment is beginning and it is only natural that he should start with his church." (I Pet. 1:7, 2:12, 3:8, 4:17 Paraphrase)

Suppose you were a church member in Asia Minor in that day, afraid that you would be arrested and tortured and killed at any time. How would these answers Peter gave strike you?

"You are suffering so that your faith can be tested and refined."

"Wait a minute," you might say, "I don't *want* my faith tested and refined."

"This testing is a reminder to you to live good lives."

"I don't need to be reminded like that," you might answer.

Rabbi Kushner evaluates answers such as these in his book. Peter's answers are logical and orderly, and they have been echoed by theologians and philosophers ever since. Scholars call it the problem of "theodicy," a word which means justifying the presence of evil and suffering in the world. And Peter tried that approach. He gave proper and careful answers as to why people were suffering. But somehow he began to see that the answer those Christians needed most was not *why* they were suffering, but rather, *how* they could endure it.

And so, sprinkled through his letter are words of encouragement that seek to explain how they can keep on in the face of such misfortune. ". . .brethren," he said to them, "love one another earnestly from the heart." (I Pet. 1:22) "Above all," he says, "hold unfailing your love for one another, since love covers a multitude of sins." (I Pet. 4:8) What he is saying to them is this: if in your church you can love one another, if you can find there a spirit of rich, supportive love, then you can find the strength to endure. One of the purposes of the Church is to offer all its people this mutual strengthening, and Peter offered that as an answer to the question of how they could endure their misfortune.

In many a crisis of life, we may desire to know why, but our real need is to determine how we can keep on. A girl comes home heartbroken and shares with her mother her pain. The boy she has been going with has checked out and wants nothing more to do with her. It happened all of a sudden and without warning. What can the mother do? She can give logical answers all night and all day, and the girl's pain will still be there. "Honey," the mother can say, "he's not the only pebble on the beach. There are lots of boys around, and someone else will come along." (Now that is quite true, of course, but at that moment it is irrelevant.) "Darling," the mother can say, "he's not worth crying over. He's no good, anyway." Now that may or may not be true, but it only adds to the pain of the moment. Even a boy who is "no good anyway" doesn't want her and has left. In that little moment of pain, the girl doesn't need logic; she needs love, a shoulder to cry on, an understanding heart, a sign that someone cares.

A tired father came in from the office one evening and sat down with the evening paper. His five-year-old son came bouncing in, saying, "Daddy, I skinned my knee today." The father paid no attention. "Daddy," the boy says, "I hurt my knee." More silence as the father reads the paper. "Daddy," shouts the boy, "my knee got hurt real bad." This gets the father's attention, and he says irritably to the boy, "OK,

OK, you hurt your knee. What on earth can I do about that?" The boy's answer was short: "You could have said, 'Oh!' "

In a sense, that is one of the church's functions, saying "oh" in the right way and at the right time, and Peter saw this. It wasn't clever answers those churches needed in order to survive—it was love. "Above all else, hold unfailing to your love for one another." If your churches have this, he was saying, your people will have hope, and they can endure.

Is this ancient message worth keeping? Does this 2000-year-old advice have any relevance for us? Indeed, it does! It's a different sort of enemy we face today as Christian people. The state does not threaten us with death if we worship Christ as Lord. There is no danger of imprisonment or exile. It's a different sort of enemy we face today, but our anxiety is the same.

Our enemy today is not so much the government without as the government within. It is our own desperate predicaments that bring us concern. Will our marriage hold up? What will I do if she divorces me? Why has my child gone bad? How can I help him? Why did my daughter experiment with drugs? Why won't they share more with me? Why doesn't my boss recognize my worth? How can I keep on with this terrible job another five years to retirement? Dear God, am I losing my sanity? I am so lonely. I am afraid of dying. Is there any point to bringing children into this kind of world? How can I go on?

Do you recognize our enemies today? The persons sitting around you are bothered by one or more of these problems, or they can write their own list. Careful, logical, answers can be given to every one of these problems. But most of us don't need the logical answer as much as we need the assurance that comes from being a part of a loving, supporting group where people care about us and from which strength comes.

How can you endure your own set of problems, then, and how can you help others endure theirs? "Above all else, hold unfailing to your love for one another." This is as timely and important a word to the Church today as it has ever been, because what burdens we secretly bear! How much we have to endure without others ever knowing it! How much we need support from one another!

Most of us can speak very personally of this. I can. I remember a few years ago when word came of my father's sudden illness. Four hours later, I had driven across north Texas and was home, but he was already gone—so quickly. Thus, the drama of death was played out in my family, and I saw from an unaccustomed perspective the healing love of a church at work as the circle of love there closed around my home. Someone has called it "The Sacrament of the Coffee Pot." We came home from the cemetery that Friday afternoon, and the word was passed, "Stop in for a cup of coffee." And many did. And in the circle of conversation there, we shared. The conversation went on, and after awhile, someone laughed. The first crack in the shell of grief came, and the wound began to heal.

Then, two days later, my brother and I went with my mother to her church on Sunday morning, and we could feel it again, so strongly, so strongly, the healing touch, the balm in Gilead. Yes, they brought in pies and cakes and they sent flowers, but more importantly, "above all else, they held unfailing to their love." At its best, this is what the church offers. Not just in time of death, but for all the discouragements we face in life. The church, at its best, is a place where, as Paul said, "If one member suffers, all suffer together; if one member is honored, all rejoice together." (I Cor. 12:26)

In the kind of brittle and unfeeling world we live in, I want this kind of strengthening support. I need it. I want it for my children, this supportive, gentle love. I want my ministry to be such that whatever your pain, whatever your problem, you feel it from me. I want your membership and participation here to be such that by your attitude and your compassion you create here for others a refuge in a stormy sea, a place where when others are unkind and gossipy, critical and rude, you can count on finding understanding and love.

And when I drove back to my home across north Texas after that experience, it occurred to me that this was just what Peter was talking about in that letter. Yes, trouble will come, anxiety will come, death will come, pain will come. But you can endure it and rise about it, if in the fellowship of your church the people there, above all else, hold unfailing to their love for one another and grant to one and all of us a refuge in a stormy sea.

16 REVELATION
God Within the Shadows

Suppose that when you arrived at church a little while ago, you had found a crowd of people milling about the door in a confused sort of way. Some of them were turning around, getting in their cars, and going home. Others could be heard angrily talking with one another. Some were going on into the building. When you came to the door yourself, you could see the cause of this confusion. Nailed to the door was a copy of an official government document announcing that worship of God had been declared illegal. You were sternly forbidden to enter the doors of the church.

What had happened? In our imaginary setting, a dictator had gained control of the country. Not only had he issued a decree saying that you could not worship God, but there was also an official order summoning you to proceed directly to a government building recently built in the community. There you were to participate in a service of worship recognizing the dictator as God. What would you do?

Very quickly, some of us would give explicit answers: we would tell the government exactly where to go with this sort of interference in our religion. We would refuse to worship the dictator, and we would continue to worship God. But suppose that official census lists were being checked by the authorities. Picture yourself standing before a desk as an official puts it to you straight. He doesn't care what you decide. He is telling you that you have a simple choice between worshiping the dictator or dying. It's up to you to choose. Agree to worship the dictator, go through that door, and live. Refuse, go through this door, and die. Which one, please? Hurry and decide. There's a long line waiting.

If it is difficult to imagine this, remember that about the year 90 AD, all around the Mediterranean world Christian people were facing exactly this choice: worship Caesar, or die. About the year 50 AD, Rome, looking for some way to tie together its vast and scattered empire, had come up with the idea of making religion a cohesive force. If all subjects throughout the empire could be persuaded to worship the emperor as God, then their common religion would tie them together and impose a kind of unity on the Roman world. As a result, governing the empire would become much easier.

Thus, throughout the Mediterranean world, temples were built in cities and shrines in villages and the order came down: worship the emperor as divine lord. Suppose *you* were living in Ephesus, and this order has just come to you. You stand before the door of the church trying to decide whether to go in or to stay out. Which choice do you make?

The book called *The Revelation to John* was written at precisely this moment in history to try to persuade you to hold to your faith, whatever the cost. It was written by a Christian whose name was John. He may have been the disciple John, but five New Testament books bear that name, a name as common in that day as in this. The man who wrote the book was a prisoner on the island of Patmos, some 60 miles out in the sea of Ephesus. He knew of the crisis of faith which Christians of Asia Minor were undergoing, and his desire was to persuade them that God was still supreme, that Rome was the very epitome of evil, that God would bring Rome to ruin and very soon would establish his own kingdom. John sought to do this by describing a series of visions that had come to him on the island of Patmos. It was an incredible series of visions, filled with symbols and imagery that challenge the imagination. This book is often called "The Apocalypse," and its contents called "apocalyptic" literature. That word means "unveiling" or "uncovering" and refers to the hidden messages usually presented in such literature.

This why the book is so difficult of understanding. It is a type of literature largely absent from the present day scene. All apocalyptic literature is based on certain assumptions. History is seen as being divided into two periods, with Satan and his forces controlling this present stage, but with the second stage to be controlled by God after the overthrow of the powers of evil. That transition will come with dramatic suddenness, and it is almost here. The end of this present age is to be marked by a period of catastrophe and disorder, wars, famines, and plagues.

Revelation was written by John on these assumptions. The human situation is so bad that surely God's patience is running out, and he will bring down the evil beast of Rome, and establish his kingdom of righteousness.

What does the book contain? A series of fantastic visions is the trademark of the book: the scroll with seven seals, the four horsemen of the apocalypse, the mountains burn, the stars fall, the great beast from the sea, the great war between God and Satan, and finally, the new Jerusalem is established and the reign of Christ begins.

The book is difficult of understanding because it is written in code. The Romans, obviously, would not have permitted circulation of a book that openly named Rome as the personification of evil in the world. Thus, John wrote in terms that his people would understand but the Romans would not. The result is the visions, with their symbolic beasts of many heads and their catastrophic events.

Because of this, the book of Revelation has been misused by well-meaning people through the ages. One can find in the book, allegorically, almost anything one wants to find. Whatever one's special interest or fear or prejudice, allusions to it may be found in Revelation. This is a remarkably easy thing to do with the Bible.

Preachers have never had difficulty finding biblical texts that can be interpreted to cover any conceivable subject. One pioneer preacher whose sermons usually included some references to baptism by immersion is said to have claimed that the reference in the Song of Solomon to the "voice of the turtle," is an argument for immersion baptism. Obviously, the turtle has no voice, said this preacher, and the only sound it can make is when it plunges into the water and goes "all the way under."

This is the sort of twisted thing one can do with the Revelation of John. Its generous collection of allegory and symbol offers many such opportunities. Rev. 13:18 is the motherlode. Here, the author identified the number of the beast which rose from the sea as 666. Most New Testament scholars believe that this coded reference is to Gaius Caesar, with identification made by assigning numerical value to letters of the alphabet. Given this precedent, latter day interpreters have identified the beast as the National Council of Churches, the United Nations, Adolph Hitler, Joseph Stalin, Kaiser Wilhelm, Napoleon, Genghis Khan, and others, depending on the interpreter's historical period and political or religious prejudices.

This approach represents the worst of biblical interpretation and denies the scripture its historical setting. Remember that the people of Asia Minor were facing a crisis of faith when this book was written. Would they stay loyal or not? They needed help then, there in 90 AD. How a prophetic treatment of Joseph Stalin or the National Council of Churches could have given them assistance in their time is difficult to understand. The message of the book of Revelation should not be sought from among religious crackpots with axes of bigotry and politics to grind. It is best found in the setting in which it was written.

When we let this book live in its own day, we see that the situation of the church was desperate. Rome's command that the people worship the emperor was threatening the existence of the young church. Too many newborn Christians were giving in. To resist was to incur torture and pain too great to withstand. But precisely at this moment came John's message. It was that of James Russell Lowell's majestic hymn: "One to every man and nation comes the moment to decide, in the strife of truth with falsehood for the good or evil side. Truth forever on the scaffold, wrong forever on the throne. Yet the scaffold sways the future, and beyond the dim unknown *standeth God within the shadow* keeping watch above his own."[1]

This book becomes relevant to us, then, as we recognize that the Beast warned of in the disturbing visions still wars against us.

He is within us. The fearful beast for us is not some Russian leader, or some church council, or anything else—it is, rather, sin that rises within us, the fearful beasts of pride and lust and racism and greed that come climbing up out of the swampy waters of our worst moments. Read this book and when you come to the vivid passages describing evil as a great, loathesome beast, identify it with what you have seen of the reality of evil in your own life. Someone has said of the storms of life that all the water in an ocean cannot sink a ship unless it gets inside. It is the beast inside us, destructive and corroding, that threatens our being today, and across these centuries John's message urges us to fight it and never give in.

God knows that there will be times of testing for us, times when everything that has given meaning to our lives is threatened, and we find ourselves helpless before it. This is when we forget the decorations of faith, and our prayers express the ancient hurt we feel. Bill Muehl has pointed out that in these times we abandon flowery prose and speak simply of our heart's need: "Oh, God, it hurts—take away the pain. Oh God, it's dark—send us light. Oh God, she's gone—bring her back to me."[2]

This book, born out of human despair, speaks to us when in the dark night of the soul we hurt, and like drowning persons, we clutch for something to keep us afloat. It says that there is no wrong God cannot right, no pain he cannot ease, no evil he in his goodness cannot overcome. God does stand within the shadows, but one day he will make his purpose known to all of us. And just as one day in God's slow judgment evil Rome would fall, so in his patience God will destroy all evil and bring to himself those who in goodness are faithful.

The pointed, piercing question for those in Asia Minor and for us today is the same: faced with despair, can we be faithful? Can we endure doubt and anxiety and suffering?

Embedded like a jewel in Joanne Greenberg's book *I Never Promised You A Rose Garden* is the description of a dream that came to a suffering teenager named Deborah. She had struggled through the despair of mental illness, and was beginning to win that battle. The dream brought Deborah the vision of a great hand coming to her out of winter darkness, the hand holding three pieces of coal.

"Slowly, the hand closed, causing within the fist a tremendous pressure. The pressure began to generate a white heat, and still it increased. There was a sense of weighing, crushing time. As the dream continued Deborah seemed to feel the suffering of the coal within her own body, almost beyond the point of being borne. At last, she cried out to the hand, 'Stop it. Will you never end it? Even a stone cannot bear to this limit. Even a stone. . .'

"After what seemed like too long a time for anything molecular to endure, the torments of the fist relaxed. The fist turned slowly, and very slowly opened.

"Diamonds, three of them. Three clear and brilliant diamonds, shown through with light, lay in the good palm. A deep voice called to her, 'Deborah!' And then, gently, 'Deborah, this will be you!' "[3]

If you are in pain, if you despair over the conditions of the world or some personal burden, if you sometimes think you simply cannot endure the crushing pressures of life, you need the message of this magnificent book, and it is simply this: "Truth forever on the scaffold, wrong forever on the throne, yet the scaffold sways the future, and beyond the dim unknown standeth God within the shadow, keeping watch about his own."[4]

BIBLIOGRAPHY

Introduction

1. National Radio Pulpit, February 4, 1978.
2. *The Living Bible,* Tyndale House Publishers, 1971.
3. Charles Shultz, "Peanuts." United Feature Syndicate, Inc.

Chapter 1

1. Peter Benchley, *Jaws,* Doubleday, 1974, p. 1.
2. Richard Bach, *Jonathan Livingston Seagull,* The MacMillan Company, 1970, p. 1.
3. Ernest Hemingway, *For Whom the Bell Tolls,* The Scribner Co., 1940, p. 1.
4. Christopher Morley, "No Coaching." In *The Questing Spirit* by Halford Luccock, Coward-McCann, 1947, p. 418.
5. M. Louise Haskins, from "The Gate of the Year." In *Masterpieces of Religious Verse* edited by James Morrison, Harper & Bros., 1948, p. 92.

Chapter 2

1. Gerald Kennedy, *The Preacher and the New English Bible,* Oxford University Press, 1972, p. 176.

Chapter 3

1. Anonymous. Clipped from a local church newsletter. Mimeographed.
2. Haim Ginnott, *Between Parent and Child,* The MacMillan Company, 1965, p. 30.

Chapter 4

1. W. B. Yeats, "The Second Coming." In *Poems of Doubt and Belief* edited by Tom F. Driver, The MacMillan Company, 1964, p. 205.
2. *The New Testament in Modern English,* translated by J. B. Phillips, The MacMillan Company, 1957.
3. T. S. Eliot, "Choruses from the Rock." In *Collected Poems,* Harcourt, Brace & World, Inc., 1970, p. 160-161, stanza 6.

Chapter 5

1. Robert Hamilton, "Pleasure and Sorrow." In *Masterpieces of Religious Verse* edited by James Morrison, p. 436.

Chapter 6

1. Alfred Tennyson, "In Memorium." In *Bartlett's Familiar Quotations* edited by Emily Morrison Beck, Little, Brown and Company, 1968, p. 650.

Chapter 7

1. Halford Luccock, *The Interpreters' Bible,* Vol. 7, p. 848. Abingdon Press, 1951.
2. J. Edgar Park, *The Interpreters' Bible,* Vol. 1, p. 961. Abingdon Press, 1951.

Chapter 8

1. Edna St. Vincent Millay, "Renascence." In *Masterpieces of Religious Verse* edited by James Morrison, p. 285.

Chapter 9

1. Phyllis McGinley, *Times Three,* The Viking Press, 1961, p. 134.

Chapter 13

1. Bernard Towers, *Teilhard de Chardin,* John Knox Press, 1966, p. 35.

Chapter 16

1. James Russell Lowell, "The Present Crisis." In *Bartlett's Familiar Quotations* edited by Emily Morrison Beck, 14th Ed., Little, Brown and Company, 1968, p. 691.
2. William Muehl, *All the Damned Angels.* Pilgrim Press, 1972, p. 56.
3. Joanne Greenberg, *I Never Promised You a Rose Garden,* Holt, Rinehart & Winston, 1964, p. 208.
4. James Russell Lowell. Same as Note 1.